Afton Villa

Reading the American Landscape
LAKE DOUGLAS, Series Editor

The four classical statues of Italian carved stone at the entrance to
the Ruins Garden symbolize the different themes of Afton Villa's long
history: Hospitality, the Hunt (Diana and Apollo), and Abundance.

(Photos © Tina Freeman)

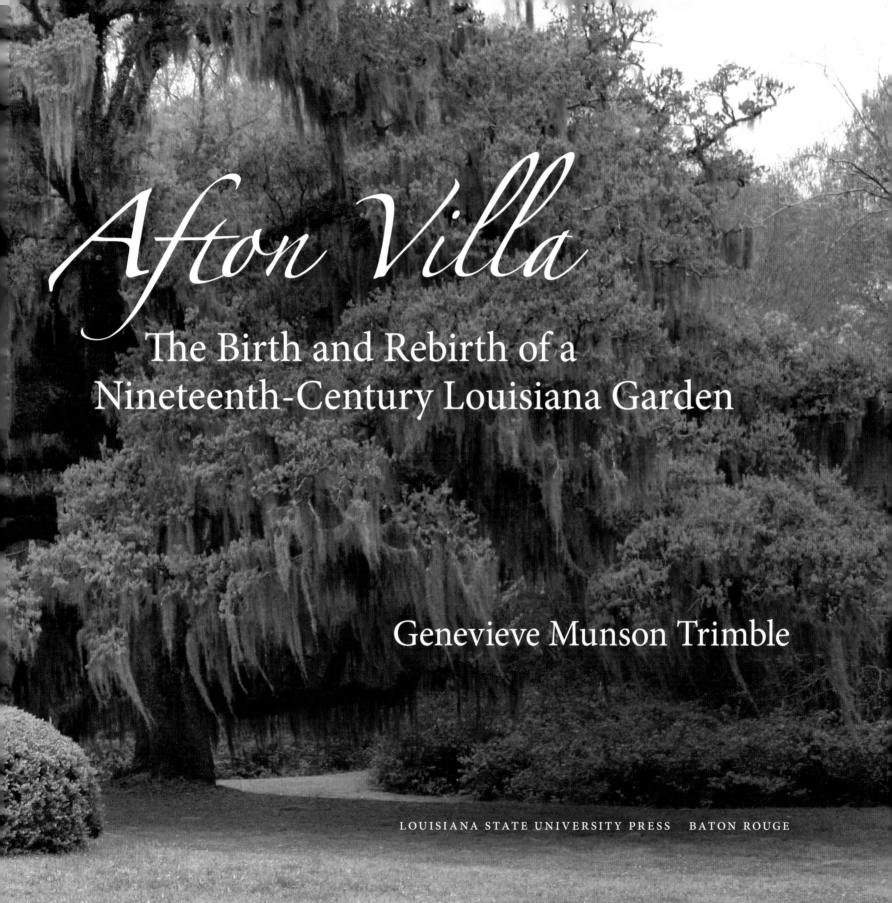

Afton Villa

The Birth and Rebirth of a
Nineteenth-Century Louisiana Garden

Genevieve Munson Trimble

LOUISIANA STATE UNIVERSITY PRESS   BATON ROUGE

Publication of this book is made possible in part by the support of the
John and Virginia Noland Fund of the Baton Rouge Area Foundation.

Published by Louisiana State University Press
Copyright © 2016 by Louisiana State University Press
All rights reserved
Manufactured in the United States of America
First printing

Designer: Laura Roubique Gleason
Typeface: Minion Pro
Printer and binder: Walsworth

Unless otherwise credited, photographs appear courtesy of Lake Douglas.

LIBRARY OF CONGRESS CATALOGING-IN-PUBLICATION DATA
Names: Trimble, Genevieve Munson, author.
Title: Afton Villa : the birth and rebirth of a nineteenth-century Louisiana
    garden / Genevieve Munson Trimble.
Other titles: Reading the American landscape.
Description: Baton Rouge : Louisiana State University Press, [2016] | Se-
    ries: Reading the American landscape
Identifiers: LCCN 2015035560 | ISBN 978-0-8071-6237-8 (cloth : alk.
    paper) | ISBN 978-0-8071-6238-5 (epub) | ISBN 978-0-8071-6239-2
    (pdf) | ISBN 978-0-8071-6240-8 (mobi)
Subjects: LCSH: Gardens—Louisiana—Saint Francisville. | Afton Villa
    Gardens (Saint Francisville, La.)
Classification: LCC SB466.U7 A388 2016 | DDC 635.09763/17—dc23
    LC record available at http://lccn.loc.gov/2015035560

For the two Morrells

A country garden encompasses much more than just horticulture and recreation, it is a matter of husbandry—a nice-sounding word, embodying concern. If you have an older property such concern is for what you have inherited—features such as old trees, ancient walls, and streams—that you care for within your boundaries, but which are a part of a much larger network.

—John Brookes, *The Country Garden*

Contents

Afton Villa

First Encounters

I do not know when it was that I saw Afton Villa and its gardens for the first time. I do remember that I was very young and that from the first time I saw it, childlike, I was enchanted. Driving down the half-mile serpentine avenue with its mysterious drapery of live oaks, rounding a turn suddenly to see the monumental Gothic villa ahead, like a fairy-tale castle with its many turrets and towers rising amidst old gardens—all of this impressed me as being one of the most romantic places I had ever seen.

During the long intervening years, Afton Villa became a landmark in my memory. Although I seldom visited it again, each time my husband, Bud, and I went by en route to his family's house in Natchez, we would invariably slow down, wave to the old gateman who always tipped his hat, and look through the gates. Afton Villa seemed always to beckon.

Then, one day in 1963, we read the heartbreaking news that Afton Villa was no more, destroyed completely by an

Afton Villa from a 1950s postcard, as I recall it looked. (Author's collection)

overnight fire, the seeming end of this famous antebellum house and of my long fascination with it. It would not be until almost ten years later, on a hot August day in 1972, that we would go through its gates again. How different it was now from the way I remembered it! The endless array of old azaleas underplanted among the live oaks were covered with vines and dieback. The heavily wooded park in the distance seemed lonely and brooding. At the end, where the avenue made its turn, there was only a shocking, gaping hole where the house once stood. All that remained were a few jagged walls, surrounding piles of bricks and stones, a huge snake-infested ruin of rubble and weeds.

Below to the left, the old parterre lay derelict, down to its bones. Only the overgrown boxwood hedge remained, raggedly outlining empty beds and spilling over the paths. The massive terraces that extended below and beyond were bleak and bare. One of them had fallen into the deep ravine, lost beyond recall. In the tiny cemetery, walled in by misshapen hedges, the tombs of the Barrows who had created Afton Villa lay forgotten.

We moved silently through the grounds from place to place, too moved to speak. Finally my husband said, "I suppose in just a matter of time someone will level all of this and put in a subdivision."

The forty-room house was gone and irreplaceable, I admitted, but the old garden could perhaps still be salvaged. "Wouldn't it be wonderful if someone were to buy this place to save this old nineteenth-century garden?" I said, little realizing that with that thought, I was committing us that day to over forty years ahead of hard work and dedication.

The Landscape's History

All old gardens are haunted, one quickly discovers, in that their former owners who have loved and tended them seem forever in the shadows, possessively prescribing and dictating what *not* to tamper with or change. Afton Villa still holds for me such ghosts of those who have come before and left indelible footprints in the garden, a constant reminder that its history did not begin in 1972 with us, the Trimbles.

It began almost two centuries ago with the Barrows, a family of Anglo-Saxon settlers from North Carolina, who migrated to Louisiana as early as 1800 when it was still sparsely settled and under the domination of Spain. In time the Barrows established a veritable dynasty of cotton plantations in West Feliciana.

History tells us that in the 1790s the land that would one day become Afton Villa Plantation was a Spanish land grant, a wilderness upon which stood a simple colonial two-story dwelling. To this place in 1820 came the last of the Carolina Barrows to migrate, Bartholomew by name, with his family, no doubt lured by the vision of wealth to be gained by the increasing demand for cotton, a flourish-

ing primary staple crop in Feliciana. Bartholomew's great-great-great-grandson, William Barrow Floyd, in 1963 published the book *The Barrow Family of Old Louisiana,* from which I learned much about the history of Afton Villa and its original gardens.

There are two intriguing stories told about Bartholomew. One written by a direct descendant states that when he came down to Louisiana from North Carolina, he brought his coffin along as part of his entourage, and the legend was that he carried all of his gold within it. This is not as macabre as perhaps it sounds since in that day caskets were frequently carried by the wealthy when traveling since the country was rough and precarious and death en route could often occur in isolated and unlikely places.

The second story is that one of the first things Bartholomew planted at his newly acquired Homeplace was a live oak that still grows today, standing somewhat apart from the other trees, at the end of the drive like a lonely sentinel now overlooking the ruins of the site where the great house once stood.

I have often wondered what Bartholomew was thinking

when he planted the little oak. Certainly not of his death, as the coffin story above might imply. On the contrary, I see him exuberant, looking ahead to the future, as one who plants a flag on a land he has conquered and claims as his own.

Bartholomew began to carve out a working cotton plantation on his newly acquired property and very soon, like other members of his family who preceded him there, began to prosper. By 1839, when he relinquished Afton Villa to his son, David, Bartholomew was a very wealthy man, and his son was soon to be considered the richest planter in West Feliciana. Strangely enough, David and his wife, Sarah, were content to live for a number of years very modestly in the 1790 house once occupied by his mother and father before him.

However, life would change. In 1846 Sarah died in childbirth, and David laid her to rest in the little woodland cemetery where his mother and other members of the family already lay.

Being a widower evidently did not suit David. One day, a year after Sarah's death, he was sitting with his daughter Mary in the lobby of the old St. Charles Hotel in New Orleans when a beautiful, well-dressed young woman passed by. It is said he told his daughter, "I am going to meet that young lady and marry her." He did. She was a widow from Oak Hill, Kentucky, who was in New Orleans visiting relatives. Her name was Susan Woolfolk Rowan.

Susan Woolfolk was all that we envision a nineteenth-century southern belle to have been. Her portrait reveals her to be handsome and stylish. Very avant-garde in her lifestyle, she loved to be first with the latest, fond of dressing fashionably and above all accustomed to living and entertaining on a lavish scale. It was not surprising that she would be less than enchanted with the simple house in the backwoods to which her husband brought her.

By all accounts, David was indulgent toward his young wife, anxious to please her. When she expressed a desire for a more elaborate house, he granted her wish, giving her *carte blanche* in the planning with but one restriction: she would leave the original house intact and merely add on to it.

At that time in the mid-1840s, the prevailing style of architecture was no longer Greek Revival, with its pristine white-columned plantation houses so in evidence along the river from New Orleans to Natchez, but rather Gothic Revival. This architectural style had gained popularity owing to a number of earlier influences—Horace Walpole, the romantic novels of Sir Walter Scott, and, probably most significant, Andrew Jackson Downing, whose *Treatise on the Theory and Practice of Landscape Gardening, Adapted to North America* (1841) strongly recommended the suitability and adaptability of Gothic Revival for rural estates.

In her travels, Susan Woolfolk had no doubt seen and been impressed by the great Gothic mansions going up along the Hudson River at that time. Nearer to Feliciana, downriver in Baton Rouge, architect James H. Dakin was building his own Gothic creation, the Louisiana State Capitol. Indeed, because of marked similarities in architectural details, some historians have surmised that Afton Villa was actually designed by Dakin. There is the curious coincidence of both Afton and the State Capitol having stepped terraces. Could this have been Dakin's idea? There is no documentation of that, nor, for that matter, any evidence of who the architect might have been.

A story comes down in family history that while the Barrows were on a grand tour abroad in France, near the city of Tours, Susan Barrow saw just the Gothic chateau she wished to copy. She imported her architect and her landscape gardener (legend says they were from France, but in all probability they were imported from up east) to supervise the task of building the house and laying out the gardens, work on which began in 1849 and took eight years to accomplish.

When she was done, Susan Barrow was true to her

Afton Villa, from an early photograph. (Library of Congress, Prints & Photographs Division, HABS LA, 63-SAIFR.V1-1)

promise: the original little 1790 house was still intact; she had simply built over it and around it. (Up in the attic, one could see the roof of the original house just a foot below the new one.) The result: a villa of more than forty rooms, a splendid turreted and towered structure, reminiscent of a fairy-tale castle, one of the largest and most unusual antebellum plantation houses in Louisiana, a notable example of eclectic Victorian Gothic architecture.

The house was built of stucco, incised to resemble blocks of stone. All of the Gothic ornamental exterior woodwork was carved from solid cypress. On either side of the house

On the right is one of the tall octagonal towers where one could climb and view the gardens below. (Library of Congress, Prints & Photographs Division, HABS LA, 63-SAIFR.V1-2)

were tall octagonal towers with parapets and copper turret guns that served as rainspouts. Family legend has it that Susan Barrow had once contemplated having a moat dug around the entire house, but thank goodness she did not fall prey to this notion; perhaps someone else reminded her of the mosquitoes in Louisiana.

Inside, the plan was equally ornate and lavish. There were rooms of every size and description: a ballroom, more Adam-style than Gothic, with crystal chandeliers and massive plaster ceiling cornices molded in a pattern of intertwined grapes and leaves; an adjoining supper room; fifteen bedrooms with dressing rooms for family and frequent guests; and the *pièce de résistance,* a spiral staircase, purported to have been designed by New Orleans architect James Gallier, which circled upward unsupported for three stories to end far above in a tower.

The doorknobs throughout the house were imported Dresden china, painted in designs of flowers and fruits with keyhole covers of French silver plate. The kitchen, unusual for homes of that period, existed within the house, down in the cellar rather than in an outside dependency. Food was sent to the dining room above by dumbwaiter.

Many of the furnishings for the house were custom-made by the renowned cabinet maker and interior designer Henry N. Siebrecht, whose shop was on Royal Street in New Orleans. Siebrecht imported other elaborate furnishings from France—paintings, floor-to-ceiling mirrors, and a collection of Victorian *objets d'art.*

The massive table in the dining room could seat over forty persons, as it often did. The bookcases in the library were wall to wall, filled with contemporary and classic volumes including the complete set of Audubon's *Birds of America* and *Animals of America,* the writings of Washington, and early American editions of Shakespeare. In short, the ambience of the interior was of the most lavish elegance and taste for the period, designed for the height of opulent antebellum living and entertaining.

Ah, but the house, a rural Victorian masterpiece of design, was only a part of the grandeur! Even more spectacular were the gardens surrounding the house: over twenty-five acres of flower gardens and pleasure grounds, extending far and wide and finally melting into the vast woodland acreage beyond the horizon.

One entered the estate through a great arched carriageway supported by massive Gothic posts. The gates were carved from solid cypress and when thrown open led the visitor into a wonderland—a half-mile-long avenue lined with live oaks, unique inasmuch as it was serpentine rather than along the more typical straight line, probably designed by the original gardener in keeping with

The spiral staircase, attributed to James Gallier, circled upward unsupported for three stories. (Courtesy West Feliciana Historical Society)

Early postcard view of the half-mile live oak avenue as it was originally, before the azaleas were underplanted. (Author's collection)

the picturesque informal landscaping popular during that period and considered suitable as an approach to a large nineteenth-century Gothic villa.

Along both sides of the graveled drive approximately 250 live oaks were planted, set in double rows very close together to form a cathedral-like Gothic arch over the driveway, thus framing a dramatic entry when one turned the bend in the road and caught unexpectedly the first glimpse of the castle-like house. In future days, gardeners would realize that live oaks planted so close together would be thwarted in reaching their natural maturity—as opposed to the many other live oaks growing freely throughout the parklike grounds, which would eventually grow in diameter to unbounded proportions.

The Villa was built upon the topmost of seven massive descending terraces carved out of the hillside by the plantation slaves. Closest to the house on the first terrace was a vast, precisely clipped boxwood parterre with gravel paths where one could stroll through an endless array of camellias, banana shrub, osmanthus, and gardenias. A picturesque summer house was set in their midst, and farther on was an intricate maze, a favorite place where the children delighted in getting lost.

Below the parterre, descending from one terrace to another, were numerous flights of stone steps, set like a great staircase. A broad graveled pathway connected the terraces and steps. Each terrace had its own special horticultural feature, flowering beds set at their edges like hanging gardens through which one could pass. On one level might be an assortment of bright perennials; on the next, a great display of roses; on another, annuals—on and on to terminate finally in the deep ravine far below.

In the ravine, Susan Barrow had her greenhouses, which supplied cutting flowers for arrangements in her house. Those greenhouses in reality resembled huge cold frames, embedded in the sides of the hill. Amidst other flowering plants in the sunken gardens were pineapple beds, a special surprise to guests. Growing pineapples was a very fashionable horticultural hobby in nineteenth-century Louisiana.

There were other terraces in the distance edged with flowering fruit trees and azaleas, luring the visitor to follow intricate graveled pathways that threaded throughout the pleasure grounds. Each path had a special name: "Long Way 'Round," "Sunny Path," "Short Cut," and even one romantically called "Lovers' Lane." All were created for leisurely exercise and the delight of giving the stroller surprise glimpses of a statue here and there, a little garden house to sit in and rest awhile, or a pond half hidden in the dense shrubbery.

When everything was completed in 1856, the name Homeplace, originally given to the plantation by Bartholomew Barrow, seemed hardly suitable for such a grand display. It was renamed Afton Villa from the song "Flow Gently, Sweet Afton" (adapted from the 1791 poem by Robert Burns and set to music by Jonathan Spilsman in 1837) that Mary, the Barrows' daughter, was known to be fond of singing as she accompanied herself at the piano.

I have no record of whether the other Barrow kinsmen in their earlier plantation houses nearby, such as Rosedown, Highland, Greenwood, and Ellerslie, were ever green with envy or haughty with disdain at such overblown Victorian ostentation created at Afton Villa. But if Susan Barrow's intention was to impress, there was no doubt that she succeeded, for her reputation as a hostess *suprême* spread throughout the region as far north as Kentucky and as far south as New Orleans. Lyle Saxon, the well-known New Orleans author, was to write of Afton Villa in his book *Old Louisiana* (1929): "This house was famous long before the Civil War, and it is said the lavish entertainments given there have never been surpassed in the South."

One of these was the Inaugural Ball in 1857 to celebrate the completion of Afton Villa. Robert Meyer, a distinguished orchestra leader and musical director of the

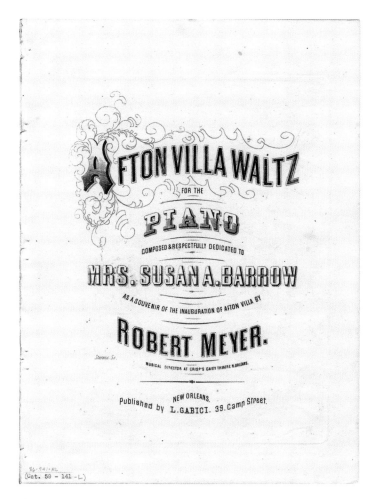

Sheet music for the "Afton Villa Waltz," composed by Robert Meyer for the Inaugural Ball in 1857. (The Historic New Orleans Collection)

Gaiety Theatre in New Orleans, composed a special musical tribute, "The Afton Villa Waltz," for that evening occasion. He dedicated it to Susan Barrow. I happily discovered a copy of this sheet of music where it resides today at The Historic New Orleans Collection.

An even more remarkable ball was held in 1857 in honor of the marriage of Batt (short for Bartholomew), David's son from his first marriage. A corps of chefs and waiters were summoned to Afton Villa to prepare the most exotic delicacies for the invited guests. For days the gardeners labored in manicuring the lawns and bringing the many flower gardens to perfection. Early on the morning of the wedding, the household staff gathered hundreds of roses and large bunches of grapes and, climbing upon ladders, draped them in garlands across the façade of the house.

By early evening, a steamboat's whistle four miles away at the Bayou Sara wharf announced the arrival of guests from New Orleans and other distant points. Horse-drawn carriages met them at the riverfront to drive them to Afton Villa. When they arrived at the entrance gate at dusk, they were astounded to discover that the half-mile drive was aglow with the light of hundreds of lanterns hung from the trees on each side. The whole front of the house and vast garden were also illuminated with candles, which gave the entire setting an ethereal look—as one guest wrote, "like a dream."

But the dream would come to an end all too soon. In reality, the days of such luxurious, carefree living were not long for the Barrows. Five years after the house and gardens were complete, the war that would bring ruin to much of the South began. Louisiana seceded from the Union on January 26, 1861. Nothing would ever be the same again.

Twice during the Civil War a retinue of Union soldiers came to Afton. The first time, as they arrived at the Gothic gates, unable to see far back through the trees, they mistook the entrance and drive as an approach to a cemetery so rode by and did not enter.

On another occasion, Susan Barrow was alone in the house with her two young children and their governess when the cry came that a detachment of Yankee soldiers was coming up the avenue. Mrs. Barrow, it is said, quietly went about the house, gathering all the large Norman door keys in a basket. When the soldiers arrived, she was standing alone at the front door. She held out the basket to the officer in charge. "Here are the keys to my house," she told him. "Please don't destroy it."

The officer was so impressed by the heroic gesture that he handed back the keys and replied, "We will not destroy your house, but we must take the horses as contraband." The late Bill Barrow Floyd told this story to me and said that his grandfather, then a boy of five, seeing that they were taking his little pony, ran all the half-mile drive crying behind the band of soldiers to the very front gates. At the gate, the Union officer in charge turned and commanded, "Give the little boy back his pony." It is a story that has come down through the generations.

The war spared the house and gardens of Afton Villa, but it did not spare David Barrow financially or physically. He died in February of 1874, during the hard days of Reconstruction, at the age of sixty-nine. Susan buried him in the small enclosed cemetery, now surrounded by the garden, beside his first wife, Sarah, near the tombs of his mother and father and other members of the Barrow family.

Susan Ann Mitchum Woolfolk, second wife of David Barrow. (From *The Barrow Family of Old Louisiana*, by William Barrow Floyd, 1963)

David Barrow, owner of Afton Villa. (From *The Barrow Family of Old Louisiana*, by William Barrow Floyd, 1963)

Rear view of Afton Villa, ca. 1915. (From *The Barrow Family of Old Louisiana*, by William Barrow Floyd, 1963)

Susan Barrow stayed at Afton for another two years. Bereft of her former slaves and the ability to maintain the plantation and house and gardens, she sadly sold Afton Villa to Judge Rufus Howell for, records show, the sum of $7,000 in 1876. A family member remarked that the price was but a little more than she would have spent on one of her lavish balls.

Susan did not return to Afton Villa again. In one of the last duties before she left, she deeded the little plantation Baptist church, founded on April 22, 1871, and its surrounding graveyard and land to her former slaves. I have a copy of that deed, which the freed slaves all signed with X's. The church is thriving to this day with a devoted congregation, minister, and choir.

Susan Barrow lived for a while in St. Francisville and died at her daughter's home in New Orleans on March 9, 1898. She was laid to rest in Lexington, Kentucky.

For a time, the Howells opened the Villa as a boarding and finishing school for young women. It had a very Victorian-sounding name: the Feliciana Female Collegiate Institute. Later, it came into the hands of A. Smith Bowman, who in 1915 sold it to Dr. and Mrs. Robert Lewis of Illinois.

By that time, the house and particularly the gardens were in a serious state of decline. Addie Lewis, Robert's wife, in a pamphlet published in 1935 during the couple's ownership, writes nostalgically about the lost grandeur of the gardens—the once-flowering terraces, the wondrous flower beds, and the winding graveled paths throughout the park, all but a memory.

But important vestiges of the gardens were still there to save. Dr. Lewis was a courageous gardener. He began the herculean task of reclaiming the terraces and park. Fortunately, the far-seeing designer of the garden in 1848, in carving out the terraces, had put an underlying network of brick drains that channeled the water down to the ravines and creek below to prevent erosion. These drains were still

functioning, Dr. Lewis discovered, and to a great extent still work today in the twenty-first century!

Dr. Lewis planted a great collection of roses on these terraces and rejuvenated the park, keeping the grounds maintained from the house to the gates. It was he who began to plant in profusion many varieties of azaleas beneath the live oaks that lined the long driveway. Some of these azaleas Dr. Lewis propagated from old specimens he found in the original garden. One of these, the oldest in the parterre, was a bright orange-red azalea peculiar to this plantation garden, and today it is known as the 'Afton Villa Red' or the 'Pride of Afton'.

I must confess when I saw the avenue in full gaudy bloom that first spring after we purchased Afton I thought, "I wish instead of this myriad of clashing colors he would have planted it all white." I could envision driving down the half mile on a twilight evening in early spring between masses of ghostlike white flowers under the gray moss-hung oaks. It would have been a spectacular sight! But actually, to be historically correct, there should be no azaleas at all. In its original state, the avenue was a serpentine drive through live oak trees laid out in the prevailing picturesque style of the period, reminiscent of an English park. But Dr. Lewis felt otherwise, employing color with a lavish hand—the white of the 'Indica Alba' azalea, the purple of the 'Formosa', the orange-red of the 'Pride of Afton', and on through various shades of pink, coral, and lavender. Would I remove them now? Never! One's ideas can change. Now I have grown to love this heady mix of color. It is, I think, reminiscent of the flamboyance of the Victorian era and a style of living that once was in full bloom with the Barrows and now has vanished and is no more.

The gardens and house were opened to the public by the Lewises until they sold it in 1945 to Dorothy Mills Noble,

The avenue in spring bloom invites the visitor to enter Afton's gates. (Photo © Bevil Knapp)

a young World War II widow who with her young daughter, Adelea, came to live there. She had fallen in love with Afton Villa, she later told me, when she was a student at Louisiana State University and had come as a tourist to visit it.

Eventually, Dot, as she was called, was to meet and marry Wallace Percy, a young bachelor from Greenwood, a neighboring plantation built in 1830 by kinsman William Ruffin Barrow. The Percys sensitively restored the old Gothic house without changing the architecture. Dot Percy purchased as many of the original furnishings as she could find, which had been scattered through the years, to bring them back to the house and rooms for which they had first been appointed.

Even the garden, once nurtured so lovingly, was rejuvenated. The Percys engaged the services of Theodore Landry, one of the few trained landscape architects in Louisiana at the time, and his wife, L. B. "Bird" Landry, from nearby Port Allen. Afton Villa under the Percys began to reflect its old glory.

But tragedy struck Afton in 1963. The original kitchen had been moved from the basement of the back wing up near the stair hall in the main part of the house. One night in the early morning hours, a fire began in that area. Summoned, the St. Francisville fire department came quickly and was able to rescue the family, huddling helplessly under the live oak in front of the house. Some of the furniture on the main floor was brought out and saved. Thinking the fire had been extinguished, the firemen promised the Percys that they would return in the morning to clean up the debris.

But the fire had spread unseen between the walls of the old 1790 house and the new Gothic villa. Just as the fire truck reached the front gates, the house suddenly exploded. Down came the three-story towers, the magnificent spiral stairway, the hand- carved cypress woodwork, and the ballroom, crumbling and consumed in fiery brilliance. The *Baton Rouge Morning Advocate* in its front-page story, sadly reporting the destruction of this famous Louisiana landmark, had as its headline "What a beautiful tragedy!" quoting the words Dot Percy uttered as she watched in anguish the demise of her beloved house.

Her husband Wallace died from a long-term illness one week later, and she moved to the gardener's cottage near the front gate.

For a long time after we purchased Afton Villa in 1972, I did not meet Dot Percy. She had remarried and was still living in the cottage which she retained at the gate. I was told that since the fire she had never gone back down the drive again to view what was left of her house and garden. When we had finally excavated the ruins, I called her one spring day and begged her to come just to see what we were doing.

She came, but most reluctantly. I remember when she arrived at the ruins she sank down on a garden bench and looked around silently for a long time, obviously overcome with emotion. "What you have done here to resurrect the garden is simply beautiful," she finally whispered. "Yes, I feel I can finally come back here at last." She did, taking her long walks almost daily to watch our progress.

Later she would ask me if she could have the wedding reception of her granddaughter, whose name was Afton, in the garden. Of course she could! It was a grand affair with over four hundred people in attendance. Great white tents were put up on the terraces for the music, dancing, and elegant supper. The bridal party arrived from the church in horse-drawn carriages. Music wafted through the garden. Candlelight was everywhere and lights were strung through the trees, recalling the memory of the past when the garden of Afton Villa had been at its prime.

Dorothy Percy died in 1990. Today, her daughter Wallace Percy Woodside and her husband reside in the cottage by the gate.

Rejuvenation Begins

As the new owners of what remained of Afton Villa in ruins in 1972, Bud and I quickly began to wonder if in our zeal of acquiring this historic place, we might have overstepped the boundaries of discretion.

Of the 250 acres that were left of this once-vast plantation, thirty acres were in open gardens and grounds, all in a state of rapid deterioration. Here was a derelict acre of boxwood parterre without a single flower in it. Everywhere were overgrown trees and shrubbery in need of heavy pruning, fertilizing, removal, or replacement.

Vines grew like a mantle over everything. The park across the ravine was knee-deep in leaves. And right in the middle with the highest visibility was the great, unmanageable, unsightly hulk of Gothic ruin, with full-grown native trees springing out from the crevices of the stones. What could we have been thinking? How could we possibly begin to tackle it?

Our first step was to engage as gardeners Ivy and James Jones, two young men who had been reared at Afton Villa and knew it well. In fact, the Jones family had lived on the grounds of the original Afton Villa plantation for many years and were longtime members of the small Afton Villa Baptist Church. With them and O. A. McKeithen, a man who became the resident caretaker, we began by carting out literally tons of debris and vines, over four hundred truckloads in all, a project that took that first fall and winter.

For the next five years, we struggled. We trimmed back trees and shrubs from pathways and clipped the wayward boxwood as far back as we dared to reshape it. We scrubbed the old marble statues and graveyard monuments. We graveled the avenue and the muddy terrace around the ruins. We began to plant flowers in the parterre.

When we finished, all of this intensive work seemed hardly perceptible. The garden still needed so much more. What it needed was professional advice and guidance!

In the journal that I have kept of the garden's month-by-month, year-by-year progress since we began, there is a significant notation for September 15, 1979: "We are here today at Afton Villa for our first meeting with Dr. Neil Odenwald of Louisiana State University, who is going to be our landscape architectural consultant from this point on."

Thus began a collaboration that has been the salvation of the garden and of us as well. I often wonder what might have happened had not Neil Odenwald come into the garden at this time. It is possible that Bud and I would have grown so discouraged that we would have abandoned it altogether.

Dr. Odenwald, on LSU's landscape architecture faculty, brought more than expertise. He brought renewed enthusiasm and a sense of practicality and direction. In our more than thirty-five years' association with Dr. O, as our gardeners now call him, we have all received the equivalent of a college education in horticulture, landscape design, and garden maintenance.

One of the primary things we found was the necessity of defining at the start a philosophy—certain principles as guidelines to govern our endeavor. The earliest and most vital determination was to recognize that Afton Villa was *not* to be a restoration but rather the preservation or conservation of a nineteenth-century garden. Two totally different concepts! No attempt would be made to re-create slavishly and accurately Susan Barrow's gardens established in 1849, as appealing as that might be. To do such a scrupulous restoration of a Louisiana Victorian garden would be quite beyond our capabilities for expenditure of energy, time, or funds.

Instead, we resolved to restore the *spirit* of the original garden, and to protect it as well. We would beautify, enhance, even superimpose our own ideas, but at the same time we would be very careful never in any way to obliterate the original footprint of the garden *or* the house. Whenever possible, we would use old nineteenth-century plants and ornamentation such as might have conceivably been contained there originally, but in the interest of practicality, availability, and maintenance, we would be willing to make substitutions, so long as they were compatible with the *spirit* of the garden.

What do I mean, one may ask, when I say the spirit of the garden? To me it means the ambiance that permeates or surrounds a garden. At Afton, I am referring to the almost indefinable aura of past grandeur and, even more than this, the ability to have sustained and risen above the rigors of unbearable tragedy.

Purists might quarrel with such overlapping of ideas upon a historic landscape. But the approach we have taken between authenticity and inventiveness is not only sensible, I have felt, but creative. Above all, we would follow a difficult directive: do not attempt anything in the garden you cannot maintain. The garden must be well kept even at the sacrifice of alluring new projects. Adhering to these principles has imposed some restraints even as it has opened up some freedoms and new horizons through the years.

Early on, Dr. Odenwald and I had mutually envisioned our approach to the revitalization of the garden to be as a series of rooms, each with its own character and design, much in the way the original house had been structured, in order to offer surprising and varied experiences as the visitor strolled through the grounds. So, too, does this book now offer an imaginary stroll for the reader through the different garden rooms we created in this historic landscape: the Ruins Garden, the Parterre, the Grand Staircase, the Pond, the Daffodil Valley, the Music Room, and the Cemetery.

The Ruins Garden

I remember clearly the words that Dr. Odenwald spoke when he came on that September morning in 1979 and stood at what had been the doorway of Afton Villa, viewing the ruins for the first time. "My! My!" he exclaimed in horror, "what are we going to do with this snake pit!"

It was indeed a question I did not want to answer. It seemed too overwhelming to be answerable. Could we just ignore it for the time being, I ventured, and go on to something else? "It would be very hard to ignore," was his succinct reply, "since it is the first of the garden one sees at the end of the drive. Remember, the first impression is always the lasting one!" Decidedly, there was no option. Then and there we began an effort to do something with the ruins.

After our first meeting with Dr. O, Bud and I made a month-long trip to England to visit gardens. One of my favorites was Sissinghurst, Vita Sackville-West's magnifi-

How to start? My first impression seemed to be an unanswerable question. (Photo courtesy Neil Odenwald)

cent garden that she had created out of the ruins of a sixteenth-century castle. I was entranced by it. As we walked through it that day, my earlier discussion with Dr. Odenwald made me think: we have genuine ruins of our own,

We began by laying out a design among the piles of stone and bricks. (Author's collection)

albeit not as large or as impressive or as old. We have no towers left, nor stunning architectural elements around which to build, but why couldn't we try to do a garden in the ruins?

Back in Louisiana, thus inspired by Sackville-West's famous garden and Dr. O's enthusiasm, we began to clean up the rubble, saving all remaining wall fragments, window openings, steps, and other architectural features that could define the perimeter and size of the house. Then, under Neil Odenwald's expert direction, we started laying out a design among the stones and bricks.

The gardens in the ruins would be divided like rooms on two levels—an upper level, which encompassed the main front entrance of the house; and a lower level reached by a surviving flight of old stone steps that led down into the large bricked area where once had been the wine cellar, kitchen, and rooms for household maintenance.

We used long garden hoses to lay and snake out the curving positions and proportions of the proposed flower beds. The native tallow trees that had sprung up from the floor of the ruins would remain, especially the largest one that miraculously had come up in the very same spot where Gallier's three-story spiral staircase had once been.

The remnants of the ballroom entrance, which hung like a balcony overlooking the ruins, would also remain, as would the steps that had once led from the supper room

down to the boxwood parterre outside. The bricks and stones that had fallen down into a large pile in the center of the lower ruins we decided should become a kind of mounded rock garden.

Our first planting was simply to cover the raw bricks, stone, and dirt with ground cover. Dr. Odenwald one day brought us a huge sack of sedum, or stonecrop, which we tucked in everywhere, even in the cracks of the old brick walls. Later came plantings of strawberry geranium, maidenhair fern, and an old rare cedar fern that came from the garden of Eudora Brown, owner of The Cottage, a nearby antebellum plantation.

Gradually, the ruins began to soften and take on the look of a garden room. We selected as our color scheme blue and yellow, with touches of white, the colors that history informed us were the original colors of the principal downstairs parlors of the Villa. Notations from my garden journal tell the stories of our plant selections:

In time, the ruins began to soften with color, blue and yellow and white in early spring, changing to lavender and pink by summer. (Photo courtesy Neil Odenwald)

Along with tulips came the introduction of wisteria, phlox, Carolina jessamine, and assorted bulbs, and a host of other blue, white, and yellow flowers. (Photo courtesy Ann Stirling Weller)

The Ruins Garden with tulips in full bloom. (Photo © Bevil Knapp)

April, 1980: New plantings for the Ruins to date—wisteria around tallow trees, asparagus (*Asparagus officinalis*), dwarf coreopsis (*Coreopsis auriculata 'nana'*), strawberry geranium (*Saxifraga stolonifera*), lavender phlox (*Phlox divaricata*), confederate jasmine, yellow Carolina jessamine (over the tower wall and back wall), hydrangeas, snapdragons, daisies, and lantana (lavender and yellow), hostas (in the towers), assorted bulbs, such as daffodils, tulips, agapanthus, and marigolds.

November 15, 1980: The rock garden is pretty well planted. Sedum is doing well. Today we began to establish hundreds of cuttings of English ivy around the back walls of the ruins and rock garden.

April 12, 1981: Yesterday we laid out the beds for the back wall garden of the ruins. I am quite pleased with the way it looks even in the rough.

August, 1981: The ruins received Dr. Odenwald's blessing. In his report he wrote, "the ruins garden is in superb condition. Remarkable progress has been made in less than one year since the first plantings. The emphasis can now be on introducing old period perennials to the garden. In the future we will not have to rely on so much of one plant such as was the marigolds."

We next turned our attention to the entrance to the ruins, a problem we had never quite solved. Soon after we purchased Afton, Bud and I had taken a trip to Italy. While in Vicenza, one day I happened to see four classical statues of Italian carved stone with which I immediately fell in love. I could see them set across the ruins as a perfect remedy to soften the dismal emptiness left by the house. In my excitement I could hardly wait to bring my husband back to see my discovery.

When I described them to him, he apparently thought they were about four feet tall. Finally seeing them, he almost fainted over their size. Set upon their stone plinths, they measured over ten feet high! Scale is a hard thing to reckon with in a garden.

"How would we ever get them back to the States?" he exclaimed. "Other people manage," I said, with a confidence I didn't feel at the moment. The rest of the trip I worried over the possibility that they would be too large for the garden.

When they arrived on the wharf in New Orleans six months later and were shipped overland to Afton Villa, they miraculously proved to be just right in every dimension. They were certainly not in keeping with a Gothic villa, I admitted, but inasmuch as the Gothic villa was no longer there, the themes they represented were surely in keeping with the spirit of an old Louisiana plantation: Hospitality, the figure holding a nest sheltering a little bird; Diana and Apollo, goddess and god of the hunt; and Abundance, symbolizing prosperity. All four statues reflected different aspects of the long history of life at Afton Villa. Ten feet tall, they were in perfect scale to lift the ruins behind them to a proper height, reminiscent of the mammoth size of the forty-room house.

As beautiful as the statues were, they failed to eradicate

The statues, when installed, at once filled the sad emptiness left by the loss of the house. (Author's collection)

At last, I thought, the garden has conquered the tragedy of the ruins. (Photo courtesy Dr. Chris Werner)

the sad look of the ruins directly behind them. However, we could finally see what must be done to the entrance to the ruins.

A thriving stand of Mondo, or monkey grass, was already in place as ground cover across the terrace when we purchased Afton. We decided to leave it and gravel the muddy terrace on which the four statues stood. Dr. Odenwald suggested planting a hedge of podocarpus behind them as an entry to the ruins. Looking back, I wish I had taken his advice. The yew would have been a better

selection because of its ultimate height as a backdrop and a better texture against the statues. But yew is very slow in growing. Gardeners, I have learned, must have patience! Back in the 1970s I had not yet acquired this trait and elected to retain the privet hedge that had grown up uninvited since the fire simply because it grew so fast. The fact is it grows *too* fast and is in need of constant pruning. We have trained it in clipped square cubes, and it looks very presentable.

Across the gravel terrace we placed white boxes, reminiscent of those found at Versailles, planted with topiary cherry laurels. On the old bricked pillars that once marked the entrance to the house we placed two antique urns that we found in the garden in which we now keep flowering perennials.

Sometimes when I grow a little discouraged over some failure in the garden, I find it a boost to my spirit to look back in my journals and read how far we have come in the planting of the ruins. Eventually we introduced furniture: a long terracotta table supported by terracotta dolphins and numerous chairs and benches set about as an invitation to linger. Around the floor of the ruins, we placed pots with seasonal plantings such as tulips, petunias, and hydrangeas. On the walls, like framed flower pictures, we hung terracotta demilunes holding colorful annuals or perennials.

The records show a modest beginning of 500 pansies. We now put in 13,000 pansies of yellow, white, and blue as a ground cover each November. From 250 tulips in our first effort, we now put in 8,000 yellow and white tulips in January to come up through the pansies.

The little wisteria bushes planted around the tallow trees have grown up through the trees to make a lavender ceiling overhead. The yellow Carolina jessamine climbs vigorously over the walls as does the lantana. In the spring when all of this color is at its height, it is indeed spirit lifting to sit there for a while to survey the yellow, white, and blue profusion with the wisteria dripping down its lavender blossoms.

One day when I was sitting in the ruins, a visitor came up and asked, "Could you tell me please where the old house once was?" "Yes, certainly," I said, "you are standing in it." At last, I thought, the garden has finally embraced the ruin of what had been a tragedy.

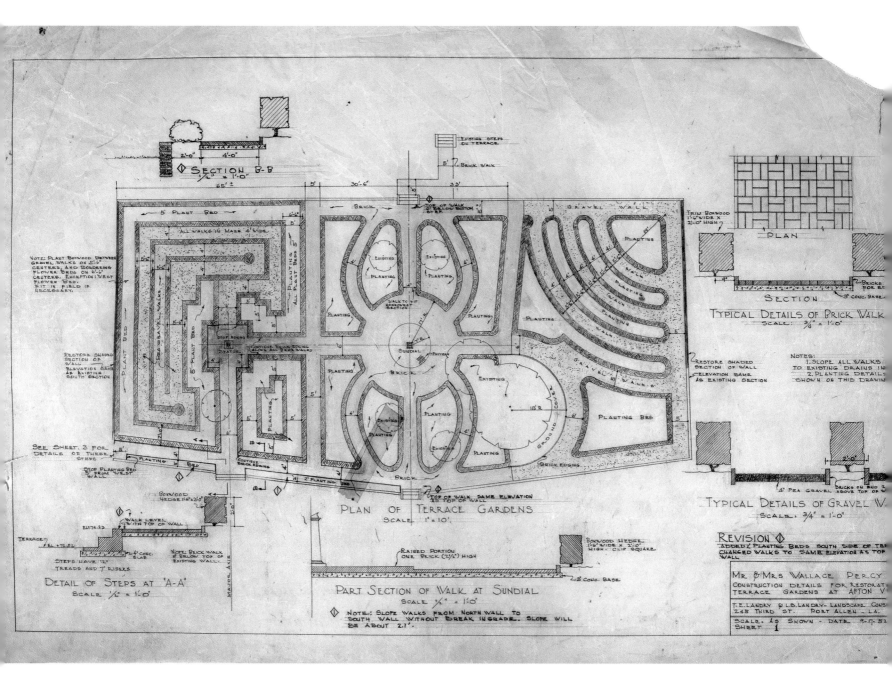

The plan of the restoration of the original parterre by T. E. Landry, 1952. (Theodore E. and Lou Bird Landry Papers, Mss. 3771, Louisiana and Lower Mississippi Valley Collections, LSU Libraries, Baton Rouge, La.)

5

The Parterre

PARTERRE: a geometric arrangement of ornamental shaped beds separated by a pattern of walks or turf areas. Variations in parterre design are unlimited, the simplest form being four beds arranged geometrically around a central ornamental feature.

—*The Garden Dictionary: An Encyclopedia of Practical Horticultural Garden Arrangement and Landscape Design* (1936)

The first terrace nearest the house overlooking the gardens below has always been a formal parterre garden. This boxwood parterre looks very much today the way it must have looked when the gardener for Susan and David Barrow first laid it out in 1848, with one exception: all paths in the garden were originally gravel, and now they are brick. Only the retaining wall that encircles the parterre is original to the garden. Over the years it has been patched and shored up. In many places, the ancient bricks are showing wear, but we have left them on purpose, primarily to reveal the wall's antiquity.

In 1955, the Wallace Percys, then owners of Afton Villa, engaged landscape architects Theodore Landry and his wife, "Bird," to do an intensive restoration of the parterre. The Landrys' plan was largely followed except for a few deviations. A sundial at the center replaced the original little garden house that, according to Dot Percy, she reluctantly removed in order to open up a more expansive vista of the gardens below. Framing the sundial were large beds outlined in boxwood and brick to contain beddings of annuals and perennials.

When we acquired Afton Villa, we found the parterre in a serious state of decline. Having suffered ten years of neglect following the fire, the boxwood hedges had grown out of bounds, much too rank and high, looking snaggle-toothed with dieback. The whole parterre had lost its pattern.

How to begin such a vast rejuvenation was beyond us. Luckily, we had engaged Dr. Odenwald at just the right time. His first advice was simply to warn us that it might be better to pull up the boxwood and replant as the only way to bring the parterre under control again. But perhaps, before such a drastic procedure, we could make one last effort to save the old boxwood. It was worth a try.

Ivy, James, and I began very cautiously to cut back. Bud was a great help also inasmuch as his favorite and most efficient garden chore was to clip hedges. Our method was to trim in stages. We began with cutting down the rank height. Using a leveler, we painstakingly took off almost a foot, as much as we thought we could without endangering the plants. Cut down to bare bones, the hedges looked horrible for a long time afterwards. When we felt they had recovered from the initial shock, we gradually began to trim the sides. It took several years before we felt we had made progress, but finally, new bright leaves began to grow and our spirits did also.

Today the boxwood is level and trimmed regularly, giving the old parterre a finished, cared-for appearance once more. We all know that the hedges are still a little too high to be absolutely correct, but we were afraid to venture more.

One of my garden friends, Anne Reily, whose mother was known for her wonderful boxwood garden at Ormond Plantation on River Road, let me in on one of her mother's secrets for cutting down on dieback: let the new growth in spring mature before giving it a clipping. We have adopted this advice and it works.

With the boxwood framework stabilized, we set out to add color. At first we planted the beds surrounding the sundial with masses of white pansies, followed later usually by petunias or white vinca. It was most impressive, but we had difficulty in keeping these four beds looking uniform because of their different exposures to sun and shade. We finally graveled the beds and put large antique urns in the

We finally graveled the four beds and put in antique urns with white flowers. (Author's collection)

26 AFTON VILLA

center of each, encircling the urn bases with dwarf hedges of boxwood. We fill the urns with petunias or the like, and within the boxwood we plant white tulips in the spring, and later, begonias or vinca. Much more successful—and much less maintenance!

The left side of the parterre (as one faces away from the Ruins Garden) is laid out in an asymmetrical pattern, with paths that curve along clipped boxwood beds containing old camellias, japonicas, azaleas, hydrangeas, and bulbs. Here grows the oldest azalea in the garden—a plant that has now grown to mammoth proportions—called the 'Afton Villa Red' or the 'Pride of Afton'. The many cuttings of this specimen propagated by Dr. Robert Lewis, one of the previous owners, in the early part of the twentieth century now exist almost as large as trees throughout the grounds.

The right side of the garden, by contrast, is set upon straight lines and features at the far end a maze that once

Another view of the parterre.

The oldest azalea in the garden, grown to mammoth size. (Author's collection)

Overleaf: The maze, a boxwood puzzle that is a special delight of children. (Photo © Tina Freeman)

The statue Flora stands on a plinth of bricks, bearing the U.S. presidential seal, which came from the White House during its renovation of 1948–52. (Author's collection)

was the delight of the children at Afton. They would look down from the tall tower of the Villa to watch with glee their playmates struggling to escape the puzzle of the intricate boxwood hedges. The maze today is still a drawing card, amusing visitors young and old.

At the entrance to the maze is a marble statue of a young girl feeding birds from her apron, one of the statues we found in the garden. Her Victorian origin is a mystery, and we call her simply Flora. She stands on a plinth of old

bricks that bear a plaque with the U.S. presidential seal and an inscription noting the bricks are from the White House. They were recovered from the original White House when it was renovated during the Truman administration (1948–1952).

If one looks down and away from Flora through an opening of clipped yew columns and sasanqua trees that leads to the descending terraces beyond, another white marble statue can be seen in the distance. These two statues on axis mark the progression of the other terraces descending to the ravine far below, beckoning the visitor to follow.

6

The Grand Staircase

It is said that when Dr. Lewis first came to Afton in 1915 to rescue these gardens, he found the terraces below the parterre used as sharecroppers' fields of corn, cotton, and potatoes. One day while working in the fields, his spade hit something hard and he suddenly realized that he had unearthed a flight of the old terrace steps. Because the far-sighted original gardener had put down a network of underground brick drains in the 1840s to combat erosion, the grounds had remained firm, and Dr. Lewis was able to laboriously slough off the fields to get back to the original contours of the terraces.

When Bud and I first arrived at Afton, the wide gravel path that once linked these terraces and flights of steps had long ago disappeared. The last terrace, the seventh, had already fallen into the ravine below. Only patchy weeds covered the once-luxuriant rolling lawns. A number of years would pass before we could realize the dream of restoring the gravel path.

A passage from my garden journal dated June 20, 1985, states: ". . . arrived at Afton last evening to meet Dr. Odenwald today for the specific purpose of laying out a large

One of the seven original terraces. (Author's collection)

We at last began to restore the gravel path that led down the terraces, 1985. (Photo courtesy Neil Odenwald)

gravel path from the Parterre Garden all the way down the terraces connecting the old flights of steps." Ivy Jones, our gardener, had rented a sod-cutter, a wonderful machine that precisely cut out the turf so efficiently that it took us but a day to accomplish this difficult task. We made an interesting discovery: beneath the sod we found soft brick, crumbly to the touch of the spade. We wondered—was there actually an old brick walk once connecting the steps? It had always been supposed that from the very beginning of the garden only gravel paths were used. It has remained an unanswered question.

A day later, the truck with the gravel arrived and the gardeners worked hard to lay it out and rake it until it was as smooth as glass. It looked unbelievably great! We wondered why we had waited so long to restore the path. We called Dr. Odenwald in Baton Rouge at 6 p.m. after it was

a *fait accompli* to give him the news. To our amazement and delight, he said, "I'm coming right now to see it! I can't wait until my next visit!" We thought he was certainly joking, but not so. He was there in an hour and was overcome with the result. It *was* astonishing how linking the parterre with the old terraces had broadened the spectrum of the garden.

On the second-to-last terrace, on a straight line with the projected path, there was a round bed framed by boxwood and centered by one of the original garden statues. I had loved her on first sight! More than seven feet tall and carved of Italian marble, her face lined by the erosion of time, and her abundant, long, wavy hair blown back as if by an invisible wind, she reminded me at once of the prow of some ancient Roman ship set out on a high sea.

We interrupted the gravel path in order to encircle this bed, then allowed it to continue on its straight line to the very edge of the last terrace overlooking the ravine below. Far down in the overgrown ravine, now filled with volunteer beech, oak, and pine, was once the setting of Susan Barrow's hothouses—where she grew seasonal cut flowers for arrangements in her house—as well as her extensive pineapple beds.

Ivy discovered in the dense undergrowth an old stone plinth at the foot of one of the beech trees, which we surmised might have once held another statue or perhaps a garden ornament. It was brought up and set at the end of the gravel path. On its top, we placed a large topiary boxwood, thus denoting the terminus of the main axis of the garden.

Beneath the ancient live oak tree just off the path near the statue, we placed a garden bench so that one could sit

One of the original marble statues—I loved her on first sight.

(Author's collection)

and look back, upward and beyond, to get a panoramic view of the terraces, the flights of old steps, the parterre, and, once upon a time, the tall towers of the Villa over the tops of the trees.

How easy to imagine it! It was a grand sight, we thought, upon finishing it. Then and there we named it the Grand Staircase.

I recall looking back down into the heavy wooded ravine below and saying to Bud, "I wish we could go even farther . . . how exciting it would be to find the remains of those hothouses and pineapple gardens."

"Stop!" Bud said. "You have gone far enough!"

But Dr. O and I had already set our eyes upon another alluring project.

Left: We placed a large pot of topiary boxwood on the plinth at the end of the path to terminate the axis. (Photo © Tina Freeman)

Above: A view of the finished path on the last terrace. (Photo © Tina Freeman)

7

The Ponds

Water is essential to a garden. I am not referring to watering the garden, but rather to the sight and sound of water in the garden.

The pond at the entrance to Afton is of unknown origin. I have often been told it was there as a watering hole for the earliest settlers in the colonial territory long before there was an Afton Villa. Situated by the gatekeeper's house, the pond is the first thing to catch the eye as one arrives at the gate. It is centered by a three-tiered nineteenth-century cast-iron fountain that I assume was placed there by Dr. Lewis or Dot Percy. Ringed with azaleas and in springtime draped by swags of the native Cherokee rose, the pond seems to promise the visitor lovely things to come beyond the gate.

But when we acquired Afton there was no evidence of water beyond, only a small creek hidden out of sight far down in one of the ravines. The ravine itself was like a ragged tear in the landscape running from the foot of the terraces, cutting the garden from view of the park beyond and absolutely impossible to keep up.

Shortly after purchasing the Villa, we decided a pond would be the first major project we would undertake. We secured the services of the local pond digger, Bo Bryan, to do the work. Mr. Bryan built up a levee across the ravine at its west end, sealing off the ravine and creating a pond as deep as the ravine itself.

When the pond was eventually filled with water, Bud and I were immediately excited by the effect and our progress. I had made an agreement with a Dr. Nettles of Folsom to trade a small cabin on Weathersby, a plantation I own in Amite County, Mississippi, for 300 azaleas to plant around the pond. I wanted 150 'Fielder's White' and 150 'Indica Alba'. Unfortunately, Dr. Nettles could get only 200 'Fielder's White' and no 'Indica Alba' at all, so he substituted 100 'Mrs. G. G. Gerbing'. They *were* beautiful plants!

Bud and I drove to Folsom to pick them up. Dr. Nettles had a young man with a truck to follow us. I wrote happily in my journal, "If the azaleas thrive, it will be truly beautiful to see their white reflection upon the pond with the

Left: The entrance pond with its cast-iron fountain is of unknown origin. (Photo courtesy Ann Stirling Weller)

We decided upon a new major undertaking, another pond far back in the gardens. (Author's collection)

added reflection of the dogwood trees behind them. We have already planted daffodils around the pond and they will naturalize and propagate. It is a long-range project which we won't see the result for a few years. A gardener has to have patience. Having it takes a lot of discipline."

How insightful that observation would prove to be! It did not take long for some of our optimism to wear off. The pond we soon decided was absolutely too small in scale for this landscape—how could we not have observed this during the digging? The levee was to have had a curved bow in it, and it should have been set much farther back. To me the pond looked as square as a box. Encircling it with the planting of the white azaleas made it seem even smaller and more of a square.

What could be done? Circumstances decided the question for us. A forewarning came in one of Dr. Odenwald's reports in 1983: "There seems to be a leak in the pond that is very serious. It is losing far too much water. It looks like it will take more than a few fingers of a Dutch boy to fix it!"

The pond had to be drained to discover that the culprit was a large stump left inadvertently at the bottom. The pond was filled again, but only months later an overnight five-inch rainstorm blew out the levee, disastrously taking all the "Fielder's White" azaleas planted across it and a little bridge as well, plunging everything down into the creek below and, as far as we knew, carrying them all the way to the Mississippi River. We never saw any of the azaleas or the bridge again.

It was evident that a restructuring of the pond would have to be done. Mr. Emile Marshiel was the next workman to come. He advised that larger drainage pipes must be put through the levee to take off the water during heavy rains, diverting the overflow into the little creek below to keep it from topping the levee.

The vertical "pitch" of the levee on the ravine side also had to be changed so that it would not be too steep. The overall square shape of the pond would be softened by creating a little peninsula jutting out into the water. The bank on the garden side of the pond would no longer have a pre-

cipitous cliff-like feeling but rather a graceful slope into the water.

We replaced the azaleas that had formerly marched across the levee, planting them in masses on the ravine side of the levee to soften the slope. All of this work would, we hoped, correct the problems with the pond once and for all. We placed a bench at the center of the levee where the azaleas had once been so one could sit and view in both directions the pond on one side and—what we had come to call the ravine—"The Valley" on the other side below.

We put white geese and white ducks on the pond, which we adored to watch and feed. Some of our visitors to the garden, however, did not share this sentiment. They complained vocally that the geese were too noisy and aggressive, often chasing and biting them. As for the ducks, they reminded us of Agatha Christie's mystery *Ten Little*

We loved the geese on the pond, but, alas, the visitors did not. (Author's collection)

Indians. Every morning one would be missing, mysteriously vanquished by some unknown assailant. We reluctantly did not replace them. It would have been like consigning them to death.

One of the last visions we had for the pond was to build a Gothic folly such as we had once seen by a pond in Europe. We would build it on the little point of land that we had created and on which was a derelict, dying magnolia tree. We engaged an architect to lay out a plan: a charming romantic Gothic ruin, just what we had envisioned, as a destination point where one could wander and sit for a spell. But when we were shown the estimated horrendous cost of construction, we decided it was going to be just that—a *folly* for us to build! The plans still reside in a drawer.

For a long time afterward, I must confess, I would sit at times on the bench on the levee and look across the pond and longingly think about the white geese and ducks. Wouldn't that have been an ideal spot, I would ask myself, to take down the dying tree and put that romantic structure as a charming spot to which to stroll.

The old magnolia must have heard me. It suddenly began to grow and flourish and put out new leaves. It now declares a thriving new life and place of its own. But I still dream of the Gothic folly and the little ducks and geese upon the pond. *Someday,* perhaps!

8

The Daffodil Valley

In 1984, we undertook the most ambitious project of all: opening up a vast eyesore, part of the heavily wooded and weedy ravine bounded by the levee of the pond.

When I presented the idea to my husband, he almost had a heart attack. "That is the most impractical thing I have ever heard you say!" he exclaimed. "That's like tackling the Grand Canyon!"

But Dr. Odenwald had a different reaction. In his report of April 1984:

> Very excited about plans for the new addition to the garden—naturalistic setting on slopes near pond. Have lots of ideas for simple, but high-value plantings visible from the hillside and equally meaningful for pedestrians in the garden. I see it as three phases: I. Layout of 30" paths as recommended on site; build bridges. II. Naturalize bulbs from the Cottage Plantation of Mr. and Mrs. Brown and other sources (need generous supply). III. Woody plant introductions such as azaleas, dogwood, halesia, oakleaf hydrangeas, ferns, irises, etc.

Ivy, his brother James, and Willie Dent, another one of the garden staff, began clearing out the ravine, which we first called the "Valley Garden," later the "Daffodil Val-

In 1984, we undertook the worst eyesore of all—the unsightly ravine. (Author's collection)

ley" after we decided to plant daffodils *en masse* because of their low maintenance. It was a long and back-breaking task. They cut out many overgrown "trash trees," laboriously clearing out heavy vines all the way from the small creek below to the very top of the hill, where one could suddenly see a spectacular view of the pond in the distance.

It was a long and back-breaking task that took months to finish. (Author's collection)

The bridges were painstakingly made by hand by our gardeners in the workshop. (Author's collection)

It took months of hard work before we could start thinking about laying out the projected gravel paths that must circle both downhill and uphill the steep slopes, connected intermittently by rustic wooden bridges. We decided to make the entry to the valley beneath a group of old cherry trees that had been planted during World War II by the then–resident gardener, James Imahara, about whom I will elaborate later. There would have to be three bridges built: the first, directly past the cherry trees; the second, farther along, crossing the creek; the third, at the very top to cross the overflow of the pond to the levee.

These bridges with handrails were made painstakingly by hand in the workshop at Afton under Ivy's direction. Still to come were the stepping stones, these too done on site by the gardeners. They were carefully set by Ivy and James between the bridges from the cherry trees down to the creek, from the creek up to the first level on the hill, then straight up to the top, where we placed a wrought-iron bench for one to rest after the long climb. Here, one could look over to see where the daffodils would one day bloom and also view the pond across the way.

A notation from my journal, January 1986, of our progress: "the valley is shaping up wonderfully. The gravel paths and the stepping stone area beyond the bridge are finished. Ivy and his helpers have made concrete stepping stones plus edging the paths with timbers before putting down the gravel." And on Saturday, February 15, 1986, I noted: "We met Neil early this morning to look at the valley, our newest creation. How beautiful it looks! What a fantastic job Ivy, James and Willie did. Dr. O seems very, very pleased and congratulated everyone. So did my husband, Bud, who admitted we had conquered the 'Grand Canyon!'" We spent time that morning laying out the last section of the walk and the last bridge connecting to the pond.

That year Ivy planted 1,000 daffodils in the valley as our first planting, a mere drop in a very large bucket. We

also transferred white azaleas from the pond to border the gravel walk to the bridge spanning the little creek. We set in large groupings of white azaleas on the levee as well as clusters of white spirea (or bridal wreath) down the slope on the valley side.

Other plantings gradually introduced have been camellias, grancy greybeard, winter honeysuckle, wild honeysuckle (wild azaleas), dogwood, tulip trees, assorted ferns, snowdrops, pseudacorus iris, and crepe myrtle trees.

Since that first planting of daffodils in the valley long ago, we now estimate that we have planted over 100,000 in all. I remember the first daffodils I planted were a collection of 'King Alfred', which then were my favorite. I did not know that in Louisiana, 'King Alfred' daffodils come up the first year and seldom show their faces again. Now, a little more knowledgeable, we choose for the valley only the daffodils we know are reliable and naturalize profusely. Here are

In 1986, I wrote in my journal, "The valley is shaping up wonderfully." (Author's collection)

Left: After being unenthusiastic at first, Bud found this bench to be his favorite place in the garden. (Photo © Tina Freeman)

what we regularly plant each year: 'Delibes', 'Yellow Sun', 'Exception', 'White Lion', and 'Silver Chimes'. Occasionally Peter Esserveld, from Swart and Company in Amsterdam where we get our bulbs, will send us a few selected ones to try for experiments.

We plant the new daffodils in mid-October. Each spring while they are blooming I make sketches and photographs of bare spots we have missed to use for the next year's planting. Ivy and the gardeners simply throw the bulbs and then plant them wherever they fall, creating a naturalistic planting. We do know that it is better to periodically dig up older bulbs and separate them, but we cannot possibly do this in such a mammoth area. Our rule: as we plant, we separate any old mature bulbs we happen to dig up and re-plant them elsewhere.

We deadhead the daffodils regularly during their blooming period, a day-to-day chore of pinching off the faded flowers. At the end we let the Daffodil Valley grow as it pleases until the foliage matures and turns brown. Then we clear the valley and let it take a rest until the next October's planting.

While once visiting the garden Sissinghurst, in England, I saw a little sign at the entrance of one area saying, "This garden is out of season." I thought that was a nice way to tell the uninstructed visitor who might not know of garden rotation, and so I copied Vita Sackville-West's sign.

In my over forty years at Afton, I consider daffodils the most satisfactory of all things in the garden. They are like beautiful, loyal friends who never impose on you and your time but never fail to appear in time, as in early spring, when the garden and things seem the darkest.

Postscript: After vigorously protesting our project at first, Bud found it to be his favorite place in the garden.

He would often sit on the bench overlooking the field of blooming daffodils toward the pond and would sometimes recite lines of William Wordsworth's poem, published in 1807:

> I wandered lonely as a cloud
> That floats on high o'er vales and hills,
> When all at once I saw a crowd,
> A host of golden daffodils;
> Beside the lake, beneath the trees,
> Fluttering and dancing in the breeze.

"When all at once, I saw a crowd, a host, of golden daffodils." (Photo courtesy Neil Odenwald)

9

The Music Room

As I have said before and often reiterate, when we are able to restore the original footprint of the garden, we do so; when we cannot, we seek to enhance, as long as we think it is in the original spirit of the garden.

Such was the case of the forlorn spot we found at the foot of the last terrace upon our finishing the gravel path of the Grand Staircase. Obviously, we reasoned, it had once been part of a small garden, situated as it was under an old live oak with a flight of steps leading now to nowhere. Perhaps it had once been the entry space downward to Mrs. Barrow's hothouses and pineapple beds in the ravine. That seemed logical. We did not hesitate for a moment to go on to create a little white garden of our own with no historical reference at all except that it utilized a bare, forbidding alcove under the oak tree and seemed to be the last piece to drop into the puzzle of leading the visitor along the onward path.

Out of a forlorn spot on the last terrace, we created a music room. (Author's collection)

Our first planting was to encircle the spot with ivy—which we liked, but it did not fare very well because the deer liked it also. Not disheartened, we went on to rim the little garden with white daffodils: 'Thalia', 'Mt. Hood', and 'White Lion'. In their midst we set four old marble cherubs playing musical instruments, encircling their bases with hostas.

These little statues are not original to the garden, but they have an interesting reason for being there. They formerly resided in one of the most beautiful, hidden courtyards of New Orleans, at Maison Montegut, 731 Royal Street in the Vieux Carré, where Bud and I lived briefly when we first came to New Orleans.

Maison Montegut was owned by Mr. and Mrs. Norman Dickson, who had a thriving antique shop on the first floor of the house facing Royal Street. Behind the façade was a large courtyard flanked by a spacious wing, which the Dicksons graciously allowed us to rent. Every morning when I would awaken and look out into the luxuriant courtyard from my bedroom window, I would see the four little cherubs playing their music, an uplifting start to the day.

In summer, there are masses of white caladiums and a Victorian bench and chairs in case one should choose to linger awhile. (Photo courtesy Ann Stirling Weller)

Later, when Bud and I reluctantly moved away, I asked Lila Dickson if she would consider selling the statues to us. "As much as I would love for you to have them," she said, "I have to say 'no.' I feel they belong here in this old historic garden."

I understood; my answer would have been the same. Although we finally moved to our own house in the Quarter, I never forgot the little cherubs nor did I ever forget the Dicksons. We were good friends until they died.

One day their niece, who had inherited Maison Montegut and all the beautiful antiques the Dicksons owned, called me. She lived in Florida and, as heir, was regretfully having to sell the property and all of its contents. "I know you and my Aunt Lila were great friends. Is there anything you might possibly want to buy?" "Yes," I said without hesitation. "The marble statues in the courtyard playing musical instruments."

When they arrived at Afton Villa, Dr. Odenwald, Ivy, Bud, and I eagerly went around the garden trying to find a proper place for them. Most of the spots were not good in scale. When we finally placed them in the new garden under the oak, they looked just right, as if they had come there on their own.

Someone later said they looked like little wood nymphs who have come up from the forest to play their music, and we called the garden from that day forward "The Music Room."

Now in early spring it is dotted with daffodils and ringed with blooming azaleas, including the wild azalea, as well as the native silver bell tree and a magnolia. We put pots of blooming white tulips underplanted with pansies around the garden and upon the steps.

In summer there are masses of white caladiums with pots of white impatiens. On the gravel floor of the garden we have placed a Victorian wrought-iron bench with matching side chairs just in case one should choose to sit there and contemplate the vista awhile.

10

The Cemetery

The last stop the visitor usually makes on a tour of Afton Villa is the cemetery, just a few footsteps off the parterre. Walled in by tall hedges of ligustrum and planted within by large old japonicas and azaleas, it forms a secret garden of its own. Often visitors ask me why the cemetery exists so close to the main gardens. The answer is that at the early date when it was created there were *no* gardens. Probably at first there was simply a footpath leading to the graves through the woodland from the original 1790 house. Later, when the parterre and formal gardens were laid out in 1848, it was enclosed, in all probability, by a typical wrought-iron fence with a gate. Later came the hedges of ligustrum, which were not the nineteenth-century planting.

Since the original owner, Bartholomew Barrow, and his family lived in the 1790 house until 1839, it is likely that some of his grandchildren who died in infancy as well as other family members were buried in this cemetery, many without markers, just clumps of violets over their graves as was the local custom. Here also lie Bartholomew and his wife, Bethia Brantley Barrow, side by side under handsome

Walled in by tall hedges, this old cemetery is a secret garden of its own, where lie the Barrows who created Afton Villa. (Author's collection)

English box tombs of marble, each inscribed with their dates of birth and death.

When we were clearing the overgrown graveyard, to our surprise we discovered another gravesite for Bethia Barrow, a simple ancient tombstone hidden under one of the japonica trees. The only explanation we could give was that since she died in 1843, before the gardens had been laid out, when Batholomew died in 1852, their children, wishing to give her a more appropriate burial place beside her husband, ordered the box tombs from Enochs, the marble firm of Philadelphia, and placed them symbolically side by side in the center of the cemetery.

Nearby, David Barrow, their son, the builder of the great house who died in 1874, lies by his first wife, Sarah, who died in 1846. Close to David and Sarah are the graves of some of their children who died in infancy, as many children did in those times from plagues of yellow and scarlet fever.

An elaborate marble obelisk that dominates the graveyard marks the resting place of David's brother-in-law, Senator Alexander Barrow. Alexander was born in Nashville, Tennessee, moved to Louisiana in 1823, and became the U.S. senator from that state in 1840. A graduate of West Point and Princeton, he married Mary Ann Barrow, the daughter of his relative Bartholomew Barrow of Afton Villa. Known as the "handsomest man in Washington," he served in the Senate from 1840 until his death in 1846. Among his close friends and colleagues there were Henry Clay, John C. Calhoun, and Daniel Webster. He was a brilliant speaker and debater, and some of his important addresses are today on file in the Library of Congress.

The funeral service for Senator Barrow was held in the U.S. Senate Chamber at noon on December 21, 1846. According to the *National Intelligence,* the Washington newspaper, all of the important figures in Washington were there, including President James K. Polk. Following the funeral, the body was moved and interred in the family cemetery at Afton Villa. The marble monument over his grave was placed there by the U.S. Congress.

There are other graves in the cemetery, and at least seven are the unmarked graves of Barrow relatives. The headstones are missing, in all likelihood victims of vandalism during the times when Afton Villa was deserted. We know the names of the deceased but not precisely where in the cemetery they lie:

- Bartholomew Barrow II, son of David Barrow (January 1, 1836–August 25, 1871)

- Martha Leonora Semple, wife of Bartholomew Barrow II (November 23, 1838–September 7, 1871)

- Joseph Barrow, the infant son of Susan Woolfolk and David Barrow (born and died ca. 1860)

- John Barrow, the twin of Joseph Barrow (born and died ca. 1860)

- William Sparks, son of Thomas Garten Sparks and Mary Jane Barrow (born ca. 1857, died ca. 1869)

- David Barrow Collins, son of Susan Elizabeth Taylor and Charles Bartlett Collins (dates unknown)

- Charles Bush Collins, brother of David Barrow Collins (dates unknown)

There are several obelisks that appear to be broken off at their tops. A visiting genealogist once told me that these were cut off purposely to signify the premature cutting off of life.

Ironically, David's second wife, Susan Woolfolk Barrow—who with her husband built the Villa and created its gardens—is not buried here but in Kentucky, her native state.

The visitor might note that some of the tombs are raised, a burial practice uncommon here in Louisiana's Feliciana region. Family history relates that the Barrows hid their silver in these raised box tombs during the Civil War for safekeeping from vandals and foraging parties of the enemy. We do not know if that actually happened, but we do know that, during the Civil War, plantation owners did what they could to preserve family heirlooms from looters and Union troops.

Apocryphal legends aside, nowhere else in the garden is there more of a sense of peace or hallowed place than here where so much of Afton Villa's origins and history lies buried.

11

Garden Animation

"What this garden needs is a little animation," Dr. Oden-wald observed one day as we sat alone in the ruins. "Because you and your husband don't live here permanently, oftentimes the visitor is alone in the garden and may sense a sterile quality to it. It would be nice to have some form of animation to bring it to life."

"What kind of animation?" I asked warily, fearing what his answer might be.

When we had first come to Afton, we had some early encounters with unwelcome "garden animation." At first we had been enchanted with the deer that abounded on the place and had even put out salt blocks at the edge of the woods to entice them into the open. This was before we began to put in the flowers. It did not take long for us to learn that deer can eat a field of pansies or hydrangeas in one night. In defense, we had to put up electric fences surrounding the flower gardens each night and spray the plants regularly—a horrendous task for the gardeners.

Nonetheless, after Dr. O's remark I became fascinated with the idea of animation. We all took a vote and settled on the idea of ducks and geese on the pond. What could

be more charming and less worry, we reasoned. The reader who has already read my account of our pond knows the answer.

Another idea suddenly came to me: what about peacocks? Nothing could be more romantic and appropriate than peacocks strolling in a nineteenth-century garden, I thought. We had seen them in many old gardens we had visited abroad.

A notation in my journal of October 28, 1981, tells the result:

> We let the three peacocks out this morning. One male, the most gorgeous bird I had ever seen! Plus two pea hens. Alas! They made for the woods and have not been seen since. I worry because they do not know what the wilds of Louisiana woods are like since they have only been at Audubon Park. We had no idea they would wander away since we had been told that after two weeks of confinement in our barn they would be content to stay close to the garden. I wonder if we will ever see them again.

Two wandered back immediately. The other pea hen was brought back a month later after a $200 reward was

Our Afton Villa geese roamed the grounds. (Photo © Tina Freeman)

posted. Another entry soon after in my journal proclaims, "The peacocks have settled down and look like they plan to stay—hooray!"

The peacocks were an instantaneous hit with the visitors, who took endless photographs of them and did not seem to mind at all their habit of perching on the rooftops of their cars or wildly shrieking at times as if someone in the garden were being murdered.

They were not so popular, however, with the gardeners

The peacocks were a great hit with our visitors but not so much with our garden staff. (Photo © Tina Freeman)

or Dr. Odenwald. "Two votes for the peacocks," he wrote in his report after one of his visits, reflecting his clients' enthusiasm. "One abstains!" he noted, recording his own vote. "Can you make them recognize that they are not welcome in this garden for lounging in the beds? What about dusting the pansies with red pepper?" he continued.

The electric fences we put up every night were hardly a barrier. Peacocks know how to fly. It was as if they thought it was a game to wait until after sunset, then fly over in the dark to have a feast. Add to that, they were most prolific. It seemed in no time at all our inventory of peacocks had reached thirteen.

General Robert Barrow, the grandson of David Barrow and commandant of the U.S. Marine Corps in Washington, had recently retired to his nearby plantation, Rosale, and he was enamored of our peacocks. He begged us to give him one or two, and to his amazement, we were very happy to give him four. He brought his truck one morning, and we ceremoniously put the peacocks aboard. He was overjoyed, profuse in his gratitude as he departed down the road. Two weeks later we spotted his truck coming up the drive with the peacocks. He and his wife, Patty, were apologetic, but the peacocks had completely denuded their garden.

One day I received an ultimatum from Ivy and his staff. "Mrs. T, you have to choose: It is either the peacocks or us!"

The "us" won the toss—the peacocks had to go. Yet I hold one lovely memory of the peacocks. Dr. Odenwald was in the garden with Bud and me, taking notes and evaluating our plantings. The three of us sat in the Ruins Garden late in the afternoon, resting and having an end-of-the-day cocktail. The last of the sun was shining on the flowers and upon the bright spring green of the boxwood and sedum.

Suddenly Rex, our elder male peacock, strutted into the garden oblivious to our presence, and climbed to the very top of the mound in the ruins and proudly posed, his wings gloriously iridescent amidst the color. It was a very special and beautiful moment and one I will always remember.

Now the animation in the garden is largely confined to our fantastic array of birds, an attraction here on our land where John James Audubon roamed in the 1820s. Though I cannot verify it as fact, I was told that the white ibis Audubon used in his *Birds of America* portfolio came from little Bayou Sara at the end of Afton Villa's original property. We also have chipmunks and squirrels, rabbits, butterflies, ladybugs, bees, frogs, lizards, egrets, and an occasional flock of resident wild turkeys. Once or twice we have even had an invasion of wild hogs that tore up the terraces.

And of course, we still have the deer, which we enjoy from afar when they come out at dusk or early morning and play like children, almost a ballet. Only occasionally do they venture up to the electrified fences. Ivy says,

"In the forty years they know me and what I will do and I know them and what they will do. We each stay in our own territory." We do not allow any hunting on the property and so it is a sanctuary for them, which I think they know and appreciate. Nevertheless, we continue to put up the electric fences every evening, and every plant that goes into the garden is regularly sprayed with Deer Stopper, a marvelous product we discovered through the developer James Messina that appears infallibly to live up to its name.

This does not mean that we do not have our animal pets. At one time we had an adorable pet fawn named Buck, whom Ivy found newborn on our compost pile. We owned for a time a Shetland pony called Cupid. And at the moment of this writing, we have a calf named Charlotte, who has beautiful eyes and resides in the pasture behind the barn. She comes running every time we call her name.

Charlotte, the calf, has become part of the family. (Author's collection)

12

Animated Occasions

In the end, we have concluded that the most reliable form of animation in the garden has turned out to be the people who come to visit.

One September day not long after we acquired Afton we received a letter from the chairman of the Audubon Pilgrimage, the annual festive event put on by the West Feliciana Historical Society in March. The letter was a gracious way of welcoming us to St. Francisville and a reminder as well that Mr. Montalvo, the previous owner who had purchased the property following the fire, had promised to allow the garden to be on the tour for the next spring and how happy the society members were in anticipation.

We were horrified. *What garden?* we asked ourselves as we looked around at the pitiful overgrown boxwood parterre, the denuded flower beds, the weeds and the vines. How could we possibly show this place to the public? But, on the other hand, how could we possibly refuse? What a terrible first impression it would make for us in St. Francisville to decline such a prestigious invitation to help raise awareness and attract friends and funds for this historic community.

At least, we decided, we had almost six months to get ready. What a scurry! I was like a newlywed who had just found out her in-laws were coming to visit on an inspection tour. We hurriedly graded the worn gravel avenue; cleaned up the azaleas; sowed winter grass to cover the bareness; planted pansies, phlox, and daffodils; and clipped the boxwood hedges. By the time March came we were exhausted but somewhat in readiness.

That frenzied effort was the beginning of our annual participation in the Audubon Pilgrimage, a highlight for us every spring. On that three-day-long weekend each year in March, we welcome usually over 2,000 people who come to see the azaleas, tulips, and daffodils in high bloom. The Historical Society is tremendously supportive. They arrange and provide for volunteer hostesses in costumes authentic to the Audubon era of the 1830s to stand in the gardens to greet visitors and give short narratives on the history of Afton Villa. People come from everywhere not only to see our gardens but the many lovely historic houses nearby that are on the tour.

Our successful association with the Pilgrimage prompted

Girls in period dress dance the maypole at Afton during the Audubon Pilgrimage in March. (Author's collection)

our decision to open our gates on a daily basis six months of the year. Our hours would be from 9:00 a.m. to 4:30 p.m. every day of the week from March 1 to July 1 and from October 1 to December 1. We excluded summer because it is too hot to wander outside in the garden and the winter months because of the capricious Louisiana weather that blows hot and cold.

We hired a permanent gateman just as was the custom back in earlier days. We charged a modest fee for adults and allowed free admission for children.

In these years we have had the garden open to the public, we have been astounded by the number of interested *and* interesting people of all ages who have come through our garden. Stellar among them have been the visitors arriving from the steamboats: the *Mississippi Queen,* the *American Queen,* and the *Delta Queen.* These beautiful riverboats, so reminiscent of the past, make regular trips up the Mississippi River from New Orleans to Memphis, stopping en route to allow their passengers to disembark at various historic places along the way. They dock in St. Francisville for a day and board buses that take them on a guided tour of the village and selected plantation houses and gardens.

If informed beforehand, I always try to be in the garden at Afton to welcome them as they depart the buses. The groups vary in size, but when they are manageable, we greet them with refreshments in the Ruins Garden. Depending on the time of day and year, we usually offer wine, coffee hot or cold, and little biscuits or cheese straws. While refreshments are being served, I give a brief overview of the garden before we take a walk around.

One of the favorite things we offer and the recipe most asked for is our cold *café au lait,* a concoction originating with Mary Frances Smart and her late husband, Lawrence, our friends from neighboring Beechwood Plantation. Here is the recipe:

Afton Villa Iced Café au Lait

Combine the following:

1 gallon of very strong coffee (we use 1½ packages of regular-grind CDM brand)

1½ quarts of Karo syrup

1½ quarts of light cream

1 gallon of vanilla or coffee ice cream

Stir well; enough for 60 people. We serve this in a large silver punch bowl with ice cream floating on top.

In October of 1988 the first annual Southern Garden Symposium was held at Audubon Lakes, later called Hemingbough, the property just outside of St. Francisville owned and developed by Arlin Dease as an event center. The symposium was organized through the inspiration of Dr. Neil Odenwald and Lawrence Smart of St. Francisville. Its purpose: to preserve and commemorate gardening in the Deep South through lectures, workshops, and a tour of local historic gardens, including those at Rosedown and Afton Villa. The primary objective from the start was to make this symposium one of the best annual educational garden programs in the country.

It has been an amazingly successful venture and draws both attention and attendance from groups throughout the South. Each year it features highly acclaimed speakers such as John Brookes, the famous garden designer from England; the late Rosemary Verey; Penelope Hobhouse; John Feltwell; and editors from such magazines as *Southern Living* and *Flower.*

Afton Villa's regular participation in this annual event is to sponsor a morning workshop in our Ruins Garden, led by regionally well-known floral and garden designers such as Norman Kent Johnson of Birmingham; North Carolina's Haskell Eargle; Ron Morgan of Oakland, California; Ralph Null of Starkville, Mississippi; John Grady Burns of Atlanta; Jim Johnson of Texas A&M; and many others, followed by luncheon in the Ruins Garden with all participants of the symposium.

The symposium has been a most generous contributor to the St. Francisville community. For example, it has established the kitchen garden at Oakley Plantation; it gives scholarships annually to the Robert S. Reich School of Landscape Architecture at Louisiana State University; it purchased a park site on Ferdinand Street in St. Francisville and designed a park and water feature, which it maintains.

In autumn and spring we have had individual tours too varied and many to recount, but a few have included excursions organized by the New York Botanical Garden, the Garden Club of America, the Garden Conservancy, the Smithsonian Institution, the Colonial Dames of America, and numerous garden clubs. The Southern Garden History Society gave us a swamp rose (*Rosa palustris*) as a parting gift of appreciation, and we planted it in a corner of the parterre in 1991 as a lovely memory of their visit.

One of the unexpected joys of animation has been the increasing use of the gardens for weddings. We always warn the young couples when they request to be married in the garden that we have no large shelters in case of inclement weather. This does not seem to faze most of them. They are usually agreeable to renting a tent or tents if necessary. My wonderful daughter, Morrell, who is so good at managing events, takes all this in stride. She takes the reservations, sometimes a year in advance; she gives advice on vendors, suggests appropriate sites on the grounds, and along with Ivy follows up on all details—cool and collected. On the day of the event, I am always more nervous than the bride or the groom! In all, we have had weddings with as many as 600 and as few as four guests in attendance. There are also hundreds of brides who have had their wedding portraits photographed in our garden, particularly in spring when the azaleas, tulips, daffodils, and delphiniums are in bloom.

Not so long ago, a young man in the midst of a very large group of visitors in the garden suddenly dropped down on his knees and unexpectedly proposed to his girlfriend, presenting her with a diamond ring that she happily accepted.

James DelPrince, professor of horticulture at Mississippi State University, gives a floral demonstration to the audience in the Ruins Garden during the annual Southern Garden Symposium. (Photo © Bevil Knapp)

It was too much for the little ring bearer at this wedding! Note the boy asleep on the bench. (Author's collection)

Oblivious to the amazed spectators, the couple eagerly embraced. "We will be back to have our wedding here in a few months," he unabashedly announced to everyone. And they did come back! Their wedding was very small, only a few witnesses, and took place in the Music Room Garden amidst the marble cherubs playing their instruments.

"You were right, Dr. O," I thought, as I looked on from a distance. This garden does need animation to make it come alive. All things considered, however, the humans are far less complicated than the animals.

One of my special joys is meeting visitors who come into the garden. (Author's collection)

13

Ornamentation

I am addicted to garden ornaments. Just lead me to a place where beautiful statuary, fabulous urns and containers, or handsome ornamental terracotta pots are on display and I am apt to go completely wild. At the same time, I have learned as I have grown older the definition of an important word, *restraint!*

I remember a fashion icon of long ago (it might have been Coco Chanel) who advised her clients, "Before you leave the house, look in the mirror and remove the last accessory you put on." Sage advice, not often taken. Oftentimes, less *is* more! One wonderful piece placed in a garden as a focal point in just the right place is enough, much more impressive than too many things vying for the eye of the beholder.

Another thing I have learned about ornamentation is the word *appropriateness.* Pink flamingoes strolling in a garden in Florida might get by, but they will not be right

This old stone basket that came from my mother's garden is one of my favorites. (Author's collection)

in a garden in the hills of St. Francisville. Good taste *is* suitability.

Meaningful ornamentation translates the intention and the spirit of the garden wherein it exists. One might quarrel on that basis with the four Italian statues that we have set across the front of the ruins at Afton Villa. Would they have likely been there in the first place across the façade of a Gothic Revival mansion? No, they would not have indeed. But since the house was no longer there, we felt they were in the right scale and appropriate to stand across

the ruins, not only giving height but also symbolizing the themes of Afton Villa's fabled past.

Other than these four, we have on the whole been spartan in the use of statues in the garden, leaving those that were there from the beginning and introducing only the four musical cherubs in the Music Room, which we felt seemed right in their woodland setting.

However, when it comes to our use of pots and containers in the garden, that is another story! There is a red-flag warning in one of Dr. Odenwald's reports in 1980: "We are

Just three colorful pots can make a difference. (Photo courtesy Dr. Chris Werner)

Why do we want so many pots? For no better reason than Ivy loves them. It is his favorite garden passion and chore.

going to have to cut down on pots in the garden. Too much time and labor are being used in watering and caring for 90 potted plants." And then, after a terrible freeze in 1982, another admonition: "Most of those pots in the garden look like they have been in the line of firing of machine guns!"

In 1980, we had 90 pots. Today we estimate that we have over 250, counting those in the garden and in our nursery. We know better than to go against Dr. O's advice (and we seldom do). However, one might say once you have "gone to pot," it is very hard to make a comeback.

Why do we want so many pots? For no better reason than Ivy loves them. It is his favorite garden passion and chore, to which he looks forward from season to season. I confess I have been enamored as well and have found them extremely useful for both their portability and their versatility in the rotation of design color. Potted flowers are indispensable as an immediate remedy in rescuing and bringing to life a boring spot or hole in the garden. Just place three colorful pots—or any other odd number—across a bare, uninteresting wall, or put them down on some indifferent garden steps and see the instantaneous transformation!

There is no question pots are time consuming and laborious. We have a rule, sometimes overlooked, that the moment a pot overstays its time in the garden, out it goes. It is necessary to have a backlog in the nursery area to replace it.

Ivy begins planting his spring tulip pots long before the blooming time, on or about January 12, when they arrive from the cold-storage plant. He starts with clean 16-inch clay pots in which he places pea gravel or broken chards of clay at the bottom for drainage; then he fills them with good soil. He plants the tulip bulbs at the proper depth (depending on the size of the bulbs), covers them with soil, and finishes the pots at the top with a thick planting of pansies that he has held in flats for this purpose. He then submerges all pots in a mixture of water and liquid fertilizer (he prefers Peters Fertilizer) and holds them down until, he says, "the soil stops bubbling." He dips or feeds or sprays all pots in the gardens on a regular basis with the Peters mixture.

We do a number of color variations: yellow tulips underplanted with yellow Mammoth pansies; yellow tulips underplanted with blue pansies; white tulips underplanted with white or yellow pansies. We use the variations of white, yellow, and blue to conform to the color scheme of the Ruins Garden in spring. When the tulips sprout

Ivy and Dr. O plant bulbs and spring flowers in pots. (Author's collection)

Right: An array of potted tulips and petunias can be eye-catching in an otherwise empty space. (Photo © Tina Freeman)

Permanent topiary evergreens in our Caisses de Versailles are a unifying element on the grounds.

through the undercover of pansies, they are ready to be brought out into the garden to be placed in various needed spots. Also in spring, we use pots of geraniums in the gardens and terraces and even hang them in demilune baskets on the façade of the barn. They are prepared for planting in the same way as the tulips while introducing another color scheme: a combination of red, white, and salmon pink.

I especially like to use white in the garden. One pot of white flowers seen in the distance can make a tremendous statement. I love blue and lavender flowers also, but they are recessive colors and do not show up as well from afar.

In our large stationary containers such as Caisses de Versailles we like to put permanent evergreen plantings, including clipped topiary boxwood, yew, or cherry laurel. They give form and structure to the landscape and are a unifying element to the garden when the off-season flowers are all sleeping and the gardens laid aside.

In late spring and throughout the summer, the gardens, particularly in the ruins, give way to what I like to call a "Country Garden" look. After the more stately foxgloves and delphiniums have passed their prime, we begin to introduce an informal mix of annuals and perennials of different hues and textures.

May brings our impressive collection of hydrangeas to bloom in glorious hues of blue, lavender, and pink throughout the grounds, as well as pots of blooming plumbago, lantana in shades of yellow and purple, salvia, starbright zinnias, Louisiana irises, and agapanthus.

Along the avenue our old gardenias, as tall as trees, bloom to permeate the whole garden with a delightful fragrance. In the Music Room, all-white caladiums come alive around the marble cherubs and usually thrive to early fall.

We close the gates on July 1 for three months during the height of hurricane season and soaring temperatures. Between those hot temperatures and tropical storms, we work diligently to keep the garden abloom.

By fall, garden ornamentation takes on a bolder look with plants that have survived the long summer. (Photo courtesy Dr. Chris Werner)

By October, as we prepare to open our gates again to visitors, we introduce another color palette of bolder autumnal colors: the yellows and bright orange of marigolds and chrysanthemums, which appear in the flower beds and also thrive in pots clustered around the façade of both the equipment house and barn. We cut back longer-lived annuals for repeat blooming in early autumn. We use torenia, zinnias, and anything that has survived the long, hot summer and has the stamina to stay until we close our gates on the first of December for the winter.

Visitors to Afton quite often ask me, "What does the garden look like in winter when closed?" My invariable reply: like a beautiful woman without makeup! I could say instead: like someone who has rolled up his or her sleeves to do some hard work.

Closed gates at Afton do not mean idle hours; far from it. In some ways, during this time, we accomplish our most difficult and far-reaching tasks of upkeep and planning ahead. Only when the garden is devoid of people and events can we safely do our cutting and pruning of trees and relocation of beds without impairing the enjoyment and safety of visitors.

We repaint the garden furniture and plant containers, regravel the avenue and paths, and denude the azaleas and hedges of vines that have encroached during the growing season. Actually, this is the only time we can be sure that snakes and any other treacherous predators are hibernating.

Pots of tulips underplanted with pansies foretell the coming of spring. (Photo © Tina Freeman)

It is also a fine time for dreaming. There is really no more rewarding time of year than when Dr. Odenwald, Ivy, and I sit quietly in the winterscape to survey the garden down to its bones and with notebooks and pens in hand (and hot cups of coffee) evaluate what we have done, intend to do or never do again, recheck our orders for plant material, and imagine the miraculous rejuvenation of a coming spring when we can make the garden more beautiful than ever.

The Garden's Guardians

14

There have been many who have served as the diligent guardians of the garden in Afton Villa's long history but, sadly, only a handful are remembered by name. We do not know the name of the nineteenth-century landscape gardener, for example, who had the far-seeing vision in 1848 to lay out such a magnificent and intricate landscape of parterres, mazes, paths, and terraces to bring order to what then was only a wilderness. Nor do we know names of succeeding gardeners and garden workers who labored to keep the wilderness from reclaiming Afton's cultivated landscape. We do know, however, the names of some twentieth-century designers who worked here.

In the 1950s, there was the aforementioned talented team of the Landrys, husband and wife, commissioned by Mrs. Wallace Percy, then owner of Afton Villa, to redesign the entrance gates and gatehouse in order to conform to the new proposed state highway that would run along the entrance necessitating the demolition of many old trees. The Landrys also worked on different elements in the garden's parterre at that time.

One of the memorable head gardeners was James M. Imahara, who, with his family, moved to Afton Villa in 1950. Imahara was the son of Japanese immigrants who had come from Hiroshima to California sometime in the late 1800s. Although James was born in the United States and thus an American citizen, after the attack on Pearl Harbor he and his family were ordered to evacuate California, along with other Japanese residents, to a detention camp in Arkansas, leaving everything behind. At the end of the war, he relocated with his family to New Orleans, where he met Mrs. Percy's father and through him was offered the opportunity to work at Afton Villa.

"I fell in love with Afton Villa," he wrote in his book, *James Imahara, Son of Immigrants* (1982). "The extensive gardens at Afton Villa had been laid out in the 1800s but had been neglected for years. The grounds were a wilderness, a ruin. They [the Percys] gave me labor, a tractor and built a cottage for me. I straightened out the gardens in the two years I was there. Afton Villa I think of as my second home. My home away from home."

James's children worked along with him restoring the gardens at Afton until the family left in 1952. The

Cherry trees in the Daffodil Valley are lovely reminders of the Japanese-American Imahara family gardeners who planted them ca. 1950. (Photo courtesy Dr. Chris Werner)

cherry trees that frame the entrance to the Daffodil Valley are beautiful reminders of this diligent, successful Japanese-American family who later developed one of the largest nurseries in Baton Rouge. Walter Imahara, son of James, now carries on the family tradition and owns Imahara's Botanical Garden in St. Francisville. He often visits

Afton Villa with his childhood memories and has become a knowledgeable and valued friend.

There have also been a host of faithful gatekeepers through the long years, true guardians of the property who have protected the entrance and welcomed visitors into the garden. One of them I remember in particular from the days when Bud and I would drive by the entrance en route to Natchez, long before we even dreamed of one day owning Afton Villa. He was a dignified black man dressed in frocktail coat and tall black top hat. Known as "Uncle Melton," he would smile broadly and tip his elegant hat to all passersby, persuasively bidding them to enter. Uncle Melton became a landmark in his day, famous to all who traveled by, and was even pictured on a well-circulated postcard.

In the time I have been at Afton Villa, we have had many unforgettable gardeners and guardians of the garden. The very first who came in 1972 were the young Jones men. Ivy, now manager of the garden and my right hand, is fond of telling visitors that he was "hired by Mr. T. for two weeks to cut out vines and weeds and has been here now for over forty years." James, Ivy's brother, stayed for over twenty years. In an entry in my journal on May 6, 1993, I wrote:

> Bud and I were shocked today to have James hand us a letter giving us notice that he would be leaving at the end of May. The reason? He did not give any other than at age 40 he felt he must move on. This will be a great loss as James was very good at clipping the boxwood and hedges and had become very adept at caring for the flower beds. It is hard to find someone to replace him who knows a weed from a flower.

James often comes to visit the gardens to see Ivy and his other brother, Raymond, as well as his father, Henry. Both Raymond and Henry are beloved gatekeepers.

Other gatekeepers we will always remember: Charlie Temple, Steve Johnson, and Eddie Webb; and gardeners George Pate, Willie Dent, Ralph Jackson, Dexter Roach, and Ricky Johnson.

Finally, what must I say about Ivy, our head gardener and manager for all these years? There are two never-failing telephone calls I receive before seven o'clock every morning of the year. One is from my faithful, devoted daughter, Morrell, to check on me. She is the one who takes charge of our events, the calendar, and is always on call. The sec-

An old postcard shows Uncle Melton, famous in his time as the Afton Villa gatekeeper, ca. 1940s. (Author's collection)

What would I do without Ivy? I don't want to think about it! (Photo © 2013 George H. Long)

ond is from Ivy, wanting to know how I am and discussing plans and work in the gardens for the day.

To many of our visitors, Ivy Jones *is* the garden in one respect: he is the daily voice of the garden, giving an impromptu guided tour or information about the plants. He gives advice to prospective brides in choosing the site on the grounds for their weddings or photo shoots and is there on the spot when all such events occur. He is the avid protector of the gardens from all would-be predators, mishaps, and catastrophes.

Ivy and I have shared all the garden happenings for forty years—rejoiced together at our successes and grieved together in our sorrows and disappointments. Something I shall always remember: once when I was sad and in despair and ready to give up, Ivy said, "Mrs. T., if there's no you there's no me." People often ask me, "What would you do without Ivy and Morrell?" I don't want to even think about it, I reply.

15

The Joys of Gardening—and Otherwise

When anyone becomes as involved with a garden as I have been through the years, the garden becomes a microcosm of life itself—a little world of its own where one must take the joys, disappointments, and sorrows as they come and learn to enjoy, accept, and endure.

In my over forty years of being at Afton Villa I have experienced the entire spectrum, which numerous entries in my journals through the years record. Among the special joys of preserving and working have been these:

- The joy of bringing beauty out of ruins—like T. S. Eliot's lilacs out of the dead land.

- The satisfaction of putting down again a once-lost gravel path that can now lead to somewhere.

- The delight of being and working with Dr. Odenwald, Ivy, Morrell, and my late husband Bud, who loved this garden so much.

- The pleasure that comes in opening the garden in spring to the annual Audubon Pilgrimage and, in the fall, to the

The unveiling of the historic marker on Highway 61 in 1974. (Photo courtesy Thomas Lemann)

annual Southern Garden Symposium—and to all those who come into the garden and, in that way, into my life.

- The honor of Afton (and me) being nationally recognized in 2013 by the Foundation for Landscape Studies with its annual Place Maker Award.

The ceremony recognizing Afton by the National Register of Historic Places was an unforgettable event in the Parterre. (Author's collection)

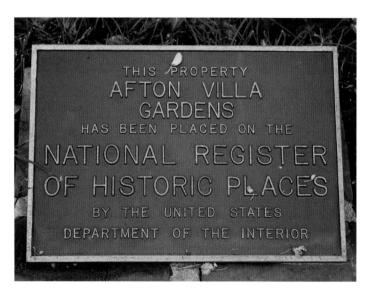

THIS PROPERTY
AFTON VILLA
GARDENS
HAS BEEN PLACED ON THE
NATIONAL REGISTER
OF HISTORIC PLACES
BY THE UNITED STATES
DEPARTMENT OF THE INTERIOR

The plaque of the National Register of Historic Places is mounted at the entrance of the Ruins Garden.

In addition, there was a very special joy on March 10, 1974, when Afton was recognized by the National Register of Historic Places, an assurance that the garden would be protected for the future. Since it came just two years after Bud and I had begun our work at Afton, it was indeed an added confirmation to us that we were undertaking a project considered worthy of note and our efforts.

It was quite a memorable affair. We erected a small tent by the Ruins Garden overlooking the parterre to serve as a podium for the speakers for the ceremony. Our numerous guests gathered as audience in the garden below.

The mistress of ceremonies was Elisabeth Kilbourne Dart, then president of the West Feliciana Historical Society and the preservation leader in the parish. After the invocation by the Reverend James C. Savoy of Grace Episcopal Church and the Presentation of Colors by Troop 61 of the Boy Scouts of America, the Honorable Davis Folkes of the Louisiana House of Representatives gave a welcoming address.

Then followed a talk by Samuel Wilson, Jr., FAIA, who was the state's preservation coordinator. A stirring recollection of "Afton Villa's Place in History" was given by William Barrow Floyd, the great-great-grandson of David Barrow and author of *The Barrow Family of Old Louisiana*. Mrs. Dorothy Mills Wilson, the former Dot Percy and former owner of Afton, spoke on "Afton's Legacy." Pamela Munson of Louisiana's Tourism Development Commission then presented to Bud and me the prestigious historic marker, which we accepted with deep gratitude. The plaque was later mounted near the steps where the ceremony took place and where it still resides today. Another historic marker denoting some of Afton's history was unveiled at the entrance on Highway 61.

As the finale, a delightful group of young Sylvan Dancers, directed by Sylvia Leake, performed a ballet in the parterre around the old sundial. The benediction was said by the Reverend George A. Nichols of First Baptist Church, and Boy Scout Troop 61 retired the colors. The event was a part of the garden's history to remember with pride and pleasure always.

There have been other joyous events worthy of recalling. It was a delight to have PBS film our garden in 2009 for a garden program that is often rerun and still seen today by television viewers.

It has also been a joy to have Hollywood occasionally come to our garden. In my journal of August 2007, I recall:

"We had a movie shot here, it was a movie based on Tennessee Williams' play 'The Loss of a Teardrop Diamond.'" That play had never before been enacted on stage, television, or in cinema.

It was a very exciting few days for us. Ann-Margret, the well-known actress, was the star, and it was such a pleasure to have her at Afton. I had always admired her on screen. Now older, past her former dancing years, she had matured into a charming, gracious lady.

A joyous movie-making for all of us at Afton. (Author's collection)

I was even asked to be an extra! (Author's collection)

What a production it was to watch! There were tents erected all over the grounds for different purposes: makeup, costume changing for the cast and extras, catering and serving generous breakfasts and luncheons for all involved.

I was even asked to be an extra! We were all costumed in vintage dresses and hats for an afternoon reception in the boxwood garden. We sat arranged in a semicircle while Ann-Margret greeted us. The scene and dialogue must have been shot and reshot a thousand times until we were all exhausted.

When the film was finally released for public showing, my part in the movie appeared but a fragment of a second, too quickly for me to utter in time, "Look! There I am!" I received no movie offers afterward, but it was fun and a joyous occasion for all of us at Afton.

16

Garden Woes

Of course a lot of our time at Afton has not been joy at all but plain hard work and worry, and often crushing defeat and disappointments, such as the time our whole crop of 8,000 tulips, for which we had been waiting for months, failed or when the levee of the pond broke, taking all the azaleas and bridges in the valley.

Even more devastating were the times when hurricanes Andrew and Gustav rolled across our property. I quote my journal entry of August 29, 1992:

This date will be etched in my mind and memory for as long as I live! I figure that Afton Villa was destroyed twice in its history. In 1963 when its great house burned to the ground. Again, on August 25, 1992, when hurricane Andrew cut a devastating path across our garden and grounds. Only time will tell us if we can ever put it back.

Bud and I met Dr. O and Ivy and Ralph at the gates. There was no way to get in other than by foot. We walked the half-mile drive back to the garden, too disheartened to speak.

There are oak trees down everywhere on the avenue, crushing the azaleas as they fall. *All* of the trees are gone in the Ruins Garden; everything smashed and leveled as if by the hands of giants.

All we can do is to begin the awesome task of cleaning up, hauling out logs and trees and leaves. It will take us forever! I am without energy, money and time to face it—and so is Bud.

Again, September 2008:

Perhaps it is best for us that we can never see ahead to what the future holds! Little could I have guessed what would happen to us on the weekend of Labor Day.

We received warning that a hurricane named Gustav was churning in the Gulf and making its way toward New Orleans, heralding another disaster like Katrina. Morrell came down from Washington and we hurriedly transferred, with Ivy and his helpers, all the furniture and rugs up to my second floor in my house here in New Orleans and closed the shutters and locked the gates and left for Afton Villa as a refuge once more.

But Gustav did not hit New Orleans as forecasters predicted. It hit *us* at Afton Villa. Catastrophe! Morrell and I huddled together through the night in our little cottage while the wind gusted over 90 miles an hour. It was terrible to hear the rattling of the glass doors overlooking the pool as if they would burst at any moment. Even more terrifying was to hear the shrieking of the trees like human beings crying out as they fell from the wind.

In August 1992, Hurricane Andrew cut a devastating path through the garden. (Author's collection)

After the storm was over Morrell, Ivy and I ventured out to see the devastation. Utter chaos! We lost in counting over 125 trees not just small trees, but ancient trees that fell as if they had been plucked up by their roots. The trees fell into the Ruins Garden smashing the flowers that we had begun to plant in anticipation of the forthcoming October Garden Symposium.

The ancient pecan tree that, along with three others, flanked the lower end of the parterre fell, smashing part of the old steps and all but obliterating one of the fine sasanqua hedges. Now only *one* pecan tree, and that badly damaged, remains of those four beautiful old pecan trees, creating a problem of too much sun on the plants, such as the hydrangeas beneath, once in shade.

Other trees fell across the pond, partially submerged in the water, their roots upended, almost 10 feet high! The bridges in the daffodil valley were smashed by both trees and limbs.

We surveyed all of this, almost weeping thinking of the coming Symposium as well as a wedding scheduled for the first of November.

More of a disaster was yet to come! Since all of our electrical power was off for a number of days, our electrical deer fences went down, enabling the deer to come in to gobble up all the flowers and foliage that were left.

During Hurricane Gustav (September 2008), the trees fell like giants, crushing the Ruins Garden. (Author's collection)

The ruin of the ancient pecan trees by Hurricane Gustav. (Author's collection)

"What on earth are we going to do?" I thought out loud in horror. Ivy, who never gives up his optimism, replied, "We are just going to pick up and go on, that's all."

He and the garden staff undertook the herculean task of clearing the rubble, determined to open the gates, if not on schedule by October 1st, at least soon afterward—which we did do on October the 6th.

While much was swept under the carpet for the Southern Garden Symposium (to be accomplished later all during the next year) I felt it was nothing short of a miracle in getting the devastated garden in some kind of presentable shape!

At such times of defeat, I am always reminded of the story of the elderly English duke who, upon seeing his magnificent alley of elms destroyed by Dutch Elm disease, ordered his gardener to replace the trees. "But, my lord," protested the gardener, looking meaningfully at his employer, who was already way past eighty-five, "it will take fifty years for those trees to mature!"

"Well then," replied the old duke, "plant them this very afternoon; you can see we haven't a moment to lose."

It seems to me that story epitomizes the necessary traits for *all* gardeners: first, wanting to leave a place more beautiful than you found it; second, the determination to pursue that goal against all odds and disappointments; and finally, always the feeling of planning and planting not just for this day but for the future.

I try to remind myself of this attitude often.

Ivy and I survey one of the 125 trees uprooted by Hurricane Gustav. (Author's collection)

Gustav spared nothing, not even the pond. (Author's collection)

17

Journaling

Of all the essential, indispensable tools a gardener needs in maintaining a garden (clippers, blowers, mowers, fertilizer, rake, etc.), one stands out for me above all others: keeping a journal.

Journaling—is there such a word? My dictionary says there is not. I hereby coin the word and proclaim there is! As one grows older, one's memory becomes the most unreliable of witnesses. Journaling keeps one on the straight and narrow path of accuracy and honesty.

I often think if only Susan Barrow had kept a journal of her garden at Afton Villa from its beginning, how much easier would have been our efforts to resurrect and preserve it. No surmising over whether or not the Villa had been built by the famous nineteenth-century architect James Dakin, as some claim it was. No wondering over the name of that first talented gardener who set out the landscape design. Mrs. Butler, who once lived at Butler Greenwood Plantation down the road, knew the name of that long-ago gardener, I've been told. But, alas, both Mrs. Butler's knowledge and the gardener himself have vanished into obscurity.

I do not know what prompted me to begin journaling at Afton Villa. Perhaps it was the knowledge that Martha Turnbull kept a meticulous diary of her garden at nearby Rosedown which became such an aid to that garden's restoration and has prompted Suzanne Turner's fine scholarly book, *The Garden Diary of Martha Turnbull, Mistress of Rosedown Plantation* (2012). I did not begin the garden journals for Afton until 1977, a full five years after we had acquired it. Would that I had started earlier! I could bring back with complete accuracy those first days in detail.

Now it is only my often-hazy memory that records the first picture of the devastating condition of the grounds and our struggles with them. Likewise, I have no written notes about our decision to engage our friend, New Orleans architect Barry Fox, to remodel the old pool house hidden away by the barn. The Percys had built this structure back in the 1940s in order to create a little pleasure pavilion for their entertainment. The renovated pool house later would become our home away from our home in New Orleans and a refuge from many a storm through the years.

When Ruthie Frierson, my close friend and a member of the New Orleans Town Gardeners, an affiliate of the prestigious Garden Club of America, first approached me in early 2008 to ask if I would consider presenting my journals to them for the Town Gardeners' Library they had established in the Southeastern Architectural Archive at Tulane University, I confess I was most reluctant—almost *embarrassed* is the proper word—to give my consent. These journals had been written so haphazardly and carelessly at times, sometimes in haste standing out in the garden in high wind and rain. I told Ruthie if I had known they would be in any way preserved for posterity and read by anyone else, there would be no incomplete sentences, split infinitives, dangling participles, or questionable spelling!

Two things eventually changed my mind. The first was my wish through the years that if Susan Barrow had left some written record when the gardens at Afton Villa were first laid out, how happy Bud, Dr. Odenwald, and I would have been in our efforts to save it. Second was my realization of how narrowly these little volumes of mine had escaped the flooding of my New Orleans house during Hurricane Katrina when we lost so many valuable family papers and photographs.

With the help of archivist Keli Rylance, the Town Gardeners reprinted my journals, handsomely binding them to incorporate colorful photographs of the gardens in different seasons. They also bound Dr. Odenwald's monthly reports that accompany the years of my journals. Now,

copies of both his and my accounts are available for future reference of gardeners and garden historians.

The reception honoring the journals' reprinting, held on November 20, 2008, was simply beautiful. Held at the Southeastern Architectural Archive, over one hundred people attended to drink a toast of champagne and to view the display of the presented books. Ruthie Frierson, chair of the journal project, and Nickie Lane, club president, gave introductory talks. Rosemonde Capomazza di Campolattaro and Ethel Clay were in charge of the reception, which included fabulous arrangements of flowers and delightful refreshments. I gave a speech of deepest gratitude to both the Town Gardeners and the Archive Library as I presented my original handwritten journals to director Keli Rylance for permanent safekeeping. Copies were later sent to LSU's Hill Memorial Library in Baton Rouge, the Smithsonian Institution in Washington, D.C., and the Garden Club of America library.

If my journals do nothing more, I hope they will bring to light to all who may read them in future days the importance of keeping horticultural records and, above all, supporting this important library project of the New Orleans Town Gardeners of the Garden Club of America in assembling and preserving such a valuable horticultural resource for the community.

As for me, I continue to keep my journal painstakingly of our day-to-day events at Afton and plan to do so as long as I am able to write and garden.

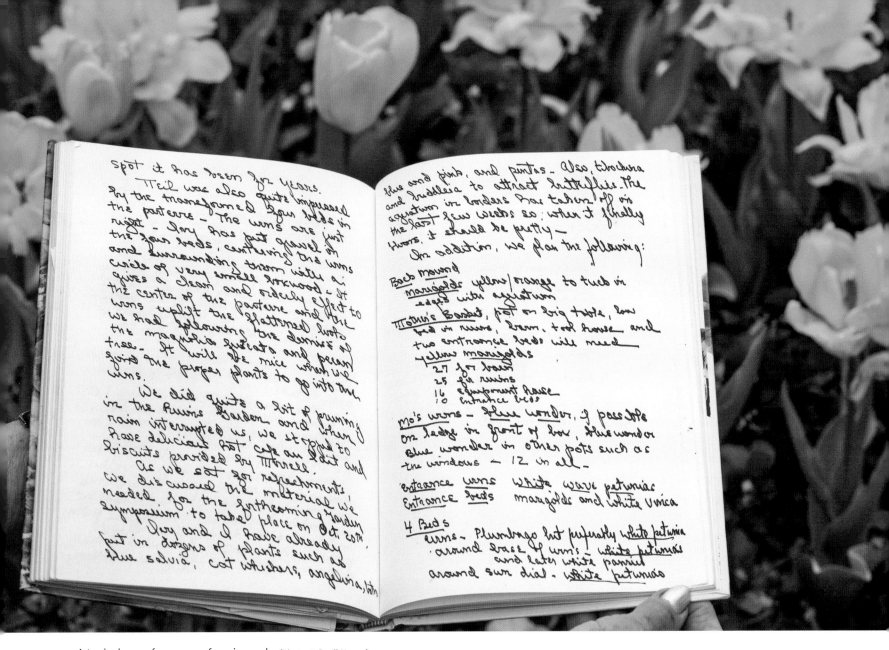

A typical page from one of my journals. (Photo © Bevil Knapp)

18

An Ode to Dr. O

I first came to know Neil Odenwald at Longue Vue Gardens in New Orleans in the 1970s when he was consultant to Mrs. Edgar Stern for her garden and I was chair of the Garden Committee. So impressed was I by his expertise and hands-on consultation that when Bud and I purchased the derelict garden at Afton Villa, I called him one day in a state of panic to ask if he would come help me. Thus began a 40-year association and friendship during which I have witnessed firsthand Dr. Odenwald's vision to transform many other gardens such as mine. In the process I have learned quite a bit about Dr. O.

A native of Mississippi, he received a bachelor of science degree in horticulture from Mississippi State University, a master of science in landscape architecture from Louisiana State University, and a Ph.D. in horticulture from Mississippi State University. He has been named a Fellow of the American Society of Landscape Architects in recognition of his teaching and service to the profession.

Dr. O was a professor at LSU, where he became director of the School of Landscape Architecture. He is a much sought-after lecturer and author or coauthor of a number of books, including *Live Oak Splendor: Gardens along the Mississippi from Natchez to New Orleans* (1992); *Attracting Birds to Southern Gardens* (1993); *The Bountiful Flower Garden: Growing and Sharing Cut Flowers in the South* (2000); and, in particular, *Identification, Selection, and Use of Southern Plants in Landscape Design* (1973), which, now in its fifth edition, is used as a textbook at LSU and many other universities, a veritable plant bible for any serious gardener.

He is the founder of the Southern Garden Symposium, held every October in St. Francisville, and its perennial master of ceremonies. With all of this, he has found time to direct the restoration and ongoing maintenance of historic southern gardens such as those at Melrose and Stanton Hall in Natchez; Rosedown in St. Francisville; the Biedenharn Gardens in Monroe; Longue Vue House and Gardens in New Orleans; and Bocage on the Mississippi River Road.

In June 1985, I wrote in my Afton Villa journal:

What an amazing and wonderful person Dr. O is. His enthusiasm and remarkable sense of humor are such that it uplifts

Dr. O directing the planting as Morrell, Ivy, and I look on.
(Photo © Bevil Knapp)

and guides our own spirits and makes this work in the garden a joy. His optimism dispels all the discouragement I sometimes feel. Just to hear him exclaim "Yes, Yes! Yes!" as he is prone to do when something in the garden delights him, banishes all disappointment that one is inclined to have.

To be a gardener demands optimism, patience and constant enthusiasm, all traits that Dr. Odenwald has in abundance. What would we do without him? We couldn't!

An ode to Dr. O!

19

Realization

I saw in Louisiana a live-oak growing,

All alone stood it, and the moss hung down from the branches;

Without any companion it grew there, uttering joyous leaves of dark green,

And its look, rude, unbending, lusty, made me think of myself;

But I wonder'd how it could utter joyous leaves, standing alone there, without its friend, its lover, near—for I knew I could not.

—From "I Saw in Louisiana a Live-Oak Growing," by Walt Whitman (1892)

My husband, Morrell (Bud), died on April 5, 2004, after a long battle with Parkinson's disease. He had fallen suddenly in the garden as we awaited a tour bus one afternoon in 1999 and broken his hip. It was the first indication of the disease from which he would never fully recover. He was unable to walk again.

Through the years that followed—the countless stays in the hospital, surgery, and the painful giving up of an active, successful life—he never complained or said, as we are often prone to do, "Why did this happen to me?" Instead, he held on to his love of family, friends, home, and the gardens at Afton Villa that he enjoyed so much.

On his rare visits to Afton, we would push him in his wheelchair through the gardens as far as the paths would let us. Overlooking the boxwood parterre, he would often recall how he once loved to clip the hedges—and he remembered especially the day in 1985 when Dr. Odenwald made a surprise presentation to him of a wonderful pair of imported pruning shears, dubbing him "a master clipper!"

Following his death, several months passed before I returned to Afton.

I remember Henry, our gatekeeper, greeted me sadly at the gates. As I drove through and looked down the avenue of oaks, I had an overwhelming feeling that I could not possibly go on with this garden without Bud. Everything about it spoke of him; even the oaks and the azaleas growing beneath them on the avenue had a somber look.

As I turned the bend where the vista widens, I stopped the car just as Bud and I always did in returning to Afton in order to admire the view that we never tired of seeing. It is a great first impression of the garden: the wide expanse of park leading downward toward the pond, the Daffodil Valley, and the terraces far beyond.

There also before me was the old oak standing alone at the very end of the drive overlooking the ruins, the one

Right: The old Bartholomew Barrow oak, planted in 1828. (Photo © Tina Freeman)

that Bartholomew Barrow, the first who claimed this land, had planted in 1828, over 175 years ago. The oak had always somehow reminded me of the lines from Walt Whitman's famous poem "I Saw in Louisiana a Live-Oak Growing." This tree, I thought, could have been just the one that inspired him!

Just to think, I realized, both this tree and the garden had witnessed a great swath of southern history. They had lived through the Civil War, the harsh era of Reconstruction, the death of the Barrows, who had been laid to rest just yards away from the oak itself in the family cemetery. Through the subsequent years, the oak and the garden had endured the days of the Depression, oftentimes neglect, the coming and going of different owners, the impacts of seasonal weather, and, finally, fire itself that demolished completely the great house, reducing it to a pile of ruins, the seeming end of Afton Villa.

But through it all, the old oak and its surrounding gardens still stood—a symbol of endurance and a triumph of nature to overcome all disasters that would befall. Wasn't this, I thought with sudden clarity, exactly what had drawn Bud and me here in the first place? It was Afton Villa's miraculous ability to have risen, phoenixlike, out of the ashes of tragedy.

And so on that sad day in 2004, seeing that old oak standing there alone, its branches covered with that mysterious resurrection fern that springs to life after a rain, and seeing my garden behind where Ivy somewhere awaited my return—seeing it all, in that strange, panoramic way, I suddenly saw and recognized myself.

I could not leave this garden behind!

I would hold on to it as long as I possibly could.

Bud and I in the Daffodil Valley, March 1999. (Photo © Starr Ockenga)

 Afterward

Long afterward, life goes on, and we still cling much to our old ways at Afton Villa. We still struggle with the same age-old problem: how far can we go in pruning and changing, undercutting the garden's evolution without sacrificing some of its history or making it sterile? The very nature of a garden is that it is a living thing. It is constantly changing and growing, subject to the effects of time, environmental conditions, and the influence of other living beings upon it.

We still adhere to our schedule of life. One of our favorite times is our traditional monthly meeting with Dr. Odenwald. We walk through the garden together, stopping to admire or criticize, deadheading here, clipping there, making notes in our journals and reports. At ten-thirty we pause for our usual ritual. Morrell or Ivy goes into the house and brings out a tray of hot café au lait and buttered biscuits with preserves. We sit down under a tree or wherever on that particular morning there is the most inviting view. And we talk about our future plans and planting and sometimes nostalgically about the past.

We all agree that we have learned more by our failures than our successes. When the tulips, daffodils, or azaleas are outstanding, we are inclined to sit back and admire. When they fail, we sit down and try to learn what went wrong and what we will do better.

Ivy and Morrell still think that I am too much of a perfectionist. Ivy will often say, "Mrs. T, can you once come into the garden and see what I have done right instead of what I have done wrong?" I reply, "Being a perfectionist does not mean that I am perfect, only that I am afflicted by always trying to be."

Now, over forty years after acquiring Afton Villa, I am sometimes startled to realize that some of the old trees at Afton and I are the very same age, our place in the landscape tentative at best, facing the same inevitable rendezvous one day with time and attrition.

Do I find that depressing? Not at all. It is this ongoing change, this overlaying of the past by the present and future, like a pattern of light and shade, a *chiaroscuro,* such as an artist might employ in painting a landscape, that gives the extra dimension to living and to preserving an old garden and makes doing so seem both worthwhile and enduring.

This being said, I must confess that sometimes on long evenings when I am alone and in a reflective mood, I have asked myself the question: why at my advanced age after all these years am I still working hard to preserve this garden at Afton? The answer, I think, is perhaps the same as to

why God first planted a garden in Eden: through love and devotion, to bring purpose and order to what might have otherwise been chaos.

I remember the late British landscape designer Russell Page (1906–1985) once said, "A garden really lives only insofar as it is an expression of faith, the embodiment of a hope, and a song of praise." Amen to that, Mr. Page!

To that, I say, *Amen!*

Over our traditional coffee and biscuits, we continue to plan and plant for the future. (Author's collection)

Acknowledgments

Here lies a paradox: while it is undoubtedly true that writing a book is among the loneliest tasks in life, it does not take long for an author to discover that one never writes a book alone. Too many voices, present and past, rush in to quicken the senses—to enlighten, inspire, encourage, and even to prod at times when one becomes disheartened.

It is difficult to acknowledge all of those who have meant so much in helping me bring this book to life. Certainly, at the beginning, I must thank Lake Douglas on the faculty in the College of Art and Design at LSU, who first came to me to suggest that I write the story of Afton Villa and its gardens. It was he as liaison to LSU Press who introduced me to acquisitions editor Margaret Lovecraft, one of the most knowledgeable, erudite, and patient of beings. Both Margaret and Lake have been at my side indefatigably all along the way. My deepest admiration as well to Catherine Kadair, senior editor, and to layout designer Laura Gleason for their meticulous attention in bringing my book to life.

My recognition must also go to a dear lost friend, the now-deceased William Barrow Floyd, who became my close confidant in the years immediately following our acquisition of Afton Villa and whose wonderfully detailed book, *The Barrow Family of Old Louisiana,* on his family's history and the beginning of Afton Villa, has been such a reliable source of information and inspiration.

I will never cease to be grateful as well to the photographers whose beautiful images of my garden illuminate my words and who have generously given me permission to use them: Tina Freeman, Bevil Knapp, the two Werner doctors, Chris and Sharon, Starr Ockenga, George Long, Thomas B. Lemann, and Ann Weller.

I especially want to recognize with gratitude the members of the Garden Study Club and the New Orleans Town Gardens, both affiliates of the Garden Club of America; to Ruthie Frierson, who spearheaded the printing and binding of my garden journals; to Bev Church; and to architect Barry Fox, who designed our little pied-à-terre on the grounds and has left an indelible imprint upon the landscape of Afton Villa.

Finally, the anonymous outside reader who was engaged by the Press to critique my book remarked in her insightful, excellent review that all the while she was reading she found herself asking a question not revealed in my text and wishing to know: how did the author get so involved in gardening in the first place?

A question that must not go unanswered! My mother, Emma Harvey Munson, was my first introduction to gardening. She loved her garden at Viewpoint, my childhood home in Houma, and had a large collection of camellias and roses, her favorites. Particularly impressed in my memory is that for over thirty-five years, until she grew too old, she supplied the arrangements for morning worship every Sunday at the little Presbyterian church. I can see her now in recollection diligently gathering the flowers from her garden on Saturday to condition them, then up early on Sunday to arrange the bouquet that my father dutifully drove into town in time to place at the altar before services began. There was no recognition of this extraordinary gift through the years, as I recall—such as the usual announcement in church bulletins, "the flowers this morning were generously given by. . . ." My mother's flowers were simply there every Sunday, a silent testimony to her continuing faith in the beauty of God's world. I confess I did not pay much attention then to my mother's devotion. It was only as I grew much older that I came to see her love of gardening and flowers as a seedling that she planted within me in my childhood that slowly, steadily grew to full fruition in my love of gardens (such as the New Orleans Botanical Garden, where I spent over twenty-five years volunteering with Director Paul Soniat, and including my own garden at Afton Villa).

To her and my father, Joseph Jones Munson, who was himself a distinguished horticulturist and sugar planter, to Morrell my husband and my only daughter Morrell, and to all others the reader will meet within the pages of this book, I offer both love and gratitude.

A SELECTED LISTING OF PLANTS IN THE GARDENS

PLANTS IN THE RUINS GARDEN

Common Name	Botanical Name	Flower Color(s)	Blooming Season
Agapanthus	*Agapanthus africanus*	Blue, white	Late spring and summer
Angelonia	*Angelonia* spp.	Lavender, blue, white, fuchsia	Late spring to fall
Blue wonder	*Scaevola aemula*	Blue to purple	Spring to fall, in pots
Boxwood	*Buxus microphylla*	(Inconspicuous)	(Evergreen shrub)
Cat whiskers	*Orthosiphon stamineus*	White, lavender	Summer to frost
Cleome	*Cleome hassleriana*	Lavender, white	Spring to freeze
Daylily	*Hemerocallis fulva*	Yellow, apricot, orange	Late spring and summer
Fern, cedar	*Selaginella pulcherrima*		(Green all year)
Fern, maidenhair	*Adiantum capillus-veneris*		(Green all year)
Foxglove	*Digitalis purpurea*	Lavender, pink, fuchsia, rose, white	Spring
Guara/Wand flower	*Guara* spp.	White, lavender	Late spring to fall
Delphinium	*Delphinium grandiflorum*	Blue, purple, lavender	Spring
Four o'clock	*Mirabalis jalapa*	Bright pink	Spring to fall
Hosta	*Hosta* spp.	White, lavender	Late spring to early summer
Hydrangea	*Hydrangea macrophylla*	Light or dark blue, lavender, white	Late spring
Impatiens	*Impatiens walleriana*	Pink, purple, white, salmon	Spring to frost
Jessamine, Carolina	*Gelsemium sempervirens*	Yellow	Spring
Jasmine, Confederate	*Trachelospermum jasminoides*	White	Late spring
Jonquil	*Narcissus jonquilla*	Bright yellow	Spring
Lantana	*Lantana camara*	Yellow, white, orange	Late spring to fall

(Cont'd)

Common Name	Botanical Name	Flower Color(s)	Blooming Season
Lantana, trailing	*Lantana montevidensis*	Lavender	Late spring to fall
Louisiana Iris	*Iris "Louisiana"*	Lavender, purple, yellow, white	Spring
Marigold	*Tagetes* spp.	Yellow, orange	Fall
Mint	*Mentha spicata*	(Not significant)	Year-round
Narcissus	*Narcissus pseudonarcissus*	White, yellow	Early spring
	Narcissus tazetta	White, yellow	Early spring
Pansy	*Viola tricolor*	Blue, purple, white, yellow	Winter to mid-spring
	Viola × wittrockiana	Blue, purple, white, yellow	Winter to mid-spring
Pentas	*Pentas lanceolata*	Pink, white	Late spring
Petunia	*Petunia × hybrida*	White, blue, lavender	Late winter to spring
Phlox	*Phlox divaricata*	Lavender, purple	Early spring
Plumbago	*Plumbago auriculata*	Sky blue	Spring to fall, in containers
Pyracantha	*Pyracantha coccinea*	White flowers; orange berries	Spring (bloom); fall (berries)
Sage, blue anise	*Salvia guaranitica*	Deep blue	Late spring to fall
Sage, scarlet	*Salvia splendens*	Scarlet	Late spring to fall
Sage, mealy blue	*Salvia farinacea "Victoria"*	Blue	Late spring to fall
Sedum/Stonecrop	*Sedum acre*	Green ground cover; yellow blooms	Late spring
Snowflakes/Snowdrops	*Leucojum aestivum (L. vernum)*	White	Early spring
Society garlic	*Tulbaghia violacea*	White, lavender	Spring to fall
Spirea/Bridal Wreath	*Spiraea prunifolia*	White	Spring in containers
Strawberry geranium	*Saxifraga stolonifera*	Green ground cover; white bloom	Late spring
Tibouchina	*Tibouchina* spp.	Deep purple	Fall
Torenia/Wishbone flower	*Torenia fournieri*	Lavender, purple, pink, white	Spring to fall
Tulip 'Golden Oxford'	*Tulipa gesnerana*	Yellow	Spring
'Ivory Floradale'		White	Spring
'Maureen'		White	Spring
'Mondial'		White	Spring
'Monte Carlo'		Yellow	Spring
'Mount Tacoma'		White	Spring
'Roi du Midi'		Yellow	Spring
'West Point'		Yellow	Spring
'White Triumphator'		White	Spring
Verbena/Homestead Purple	*Verbena × hybrida*	Lavender, purple	Late spring to summer
Vinca	*Vinca major*	Blue	Spring
Vinca, periwinkle	*Catharanthus roseus*	Pink, white, purple	Summer to frost
White flag	*Iris × germanica*	White	Spring
Wisteria	*Wisteria sinensis*	Lavender	Spring
Zinnia	*Zinnia elegans* spp.	Yellow, orange, lavender, white	Spring to fall

PLANTS IN THE PARTERRE

Common Name	Botanical Name	Flower Color(s)	Blooming Season
Azalea 'Afton Villa Red'	*Rhododendron indicum*	Red-orange	Spring
'Dorothy Hayden'	*Rhododendron hybrida*	White	Spring
'Formosa'		Magenta	Spring
'Pride of Mobile'		Watermelon red	Spring
Banana shrub/Magnolia fuscata	*Michelia figo*	Yellow	Spring
Boxwood	*Buxus microphylla*	(Inconspicuous)	(Evergreen shrub)
Calla lily	*Zantedeschia aethiopica*	White	Spring to early summer
Camellia 'Alba Plena'	*Camellia japonica*	White	Winter to early spring
'Chandleri Elegans'		Pink	Winter to early spring
'Debutante'		Light pink	Winter to early spring
'Magnoliaeflora'		Light pink	Winter to early spring
'Pink Perfection'		Light pink	Winter to early spring
'Professor Sargeant'		Red	Winter to early spring
Daylily	*Hemerocallis fulva*	Yellow, apricot, orange	Late spring and summer
Gardenia	*Gardenia jasminoides*	White	Early to late spring
Hydrangea	*Hydrangea macrophylla*	Blue, pink, white, lavender	Spring and early summer
Japanese yew	*Podocarpus macrophyllus*		(Evergreen shrub)
Live oak	*Quercus virginiana*		(Evergreen tree)
Mallow	*Hibiscus militaris*	Pink-white	Spring to fall
Mandevilla	*Mandevilla* spp.	White	Summer to late summer (in urns)
Pansy	*Viola × wittrockiana*	Blue, purple, white, yellow	Winter to mid-spring
Petunia	*Petunia × hybrida*	White	Spring and summer
Roses	*Rosa* spp.	Various	Summer to fall
Sasanqua	*Camellia sasanqua*	Pink	Fall
Swamp rose	*Rosa palustris*	Light pink	Late spring and summer
Sweet alyssum	*Alyssum maritima*	White	Spring and summer
Sweet olive	*Osmanthus fragrans*	White	Several bloom cycles, fall to spring
Tulip 'Mondial'	*Tulipa gesnerana*	White	Early spring
Vinca, periwinkle	*Catharanthus roseus*	White, pink, purple	Summer to frost

PLANTS IN THE MUSIC ROOM

Common Name	Botanical Name	Flower Color(s)	Blooming Season
Begonia	*Begonia* spp.	White	Spring
Caladium 'Candidum'	*Caladium × hortulanum*	White	Summer (leaves)
Cyclamen	*Cyclamen* spp.	White	Fall
Daffodil	*Narcissus* spp.	White	Spring
'Fortune'	*Narcissus pseudonarcissus*	White	Spring
'Mt. Hood'	*Narcissus pseudonarcissus*	White	Spring
'Thalia'	*Narcissus tazetta*	White	Spring
Hosta	*Sieboldiana elegans*	White	Spring
Hydrangea	*Hydrangea macrophylla*	Blue, white, lavender	Spring and early summer
Impatiens	*Impatiens walleriana cv.*	White	Spring to frost
Live oak	*Quercus virginiana*		(Evergreen tree)
Magnolia	*Magnolia grandiflora*	White	Late spring
Pansy (with tulips)	*Viola tricolor*	White	Winter to mid-spring
Tulip (in pots)	*Tulipa gesnerana*	White	Early spring
Silverbell	*Halesia diptera*	White	Spring
Spanish moss*	*Tillandsia usneoides*		(Not significant; silvery gray foliage)
Wild azalea (Honeysuckle azalea)	*Rhododendron canescens*	White, pink	Spring

Primary source: Neil Odenwald and James Turner, *Identification, Selection, and Use of Southern Plants for Landscape Design*, fourth ed. (Baton Rouge: Claitor's, 2006); online sources also consulted.

*Spanish moss grows on trees throughout the grounds. It is not a parasite but an epiphytic air plant. It is also not a true moss but is closely related to the pineapple and other members of the bromeliad family.

ABOUT THE AUTHOR

Genevieve "Gen" Trimble was born in Baton Rouge, Louisiana, and attended Louisiana State University, graduating with a degree in journalism. While at LSU, she met and married Morrell "Bud" Trimble of Natchez, moving to Chicago where she became a copywriter and wrote short stories for women's periodicals. They moved to New Orleans in the late 1940s after World War II, where Bud worked at a brokerage firm, rising to executive vice-president and resident manager, and Gen became active in civic affairs.

Traveling often between New Orleans and Natchez, the Trimbles knew of Afton Villa, the unique 40-room Gothic Revival plantation house in St. Francisville, Louisiana, and watched as the property declined following the villa's destruction by fire in 1963. In 1972, hoping to save the property from imminent development, the Trimbles purchased 250 acres and began rejuvenating the gardens. Working with landscape architect Dr. Neil Odenwald, they began a dedicated, lifelong stewardship of garden making, electing not to "restore" the nineteenth-century garden but rather to preserve and rejuvenate this old garden as a reflection of their own sense of garden design.

Afton is a significant regional tourist attraction for its unique garden features, including a winding half-mile *allée* of ancient oaks leading to the "garden in the ruins" of the old villa. In the spring, thousands of yellow and white tulips (up to 8,000 planted annually) and pansies fill these "ruins," and naturalized narcissi and daffodils, now numbering in the thousands, grace adjacent garden "rooms."

Gen has meticulously kept a journal of garden activities, together with personal observations of events such as Bud's death (in 2004). Like all gardeners' journals, there are rough sketches, water-stained pages, cryptic notes, and accounts of the garden's life.

In New Orleans, Gen was the founder and for twenty-five years president of the New Orleans Botanical Garden Foundation, spearheading a multi-million-dollar fund-raising campaign for its redevelopment and the construction of two signature structures, the Pavilion of the Two Sisters and the Conservatory. Following Hurricane Katrina, this garden was quickly (and completely) restored largely due to Gen's conviction that it would become a symbol of hope and community rebirth to sustain and inspire hundreds of residents returning to find little left of their pre-Katrina lives.

Gen has received numerous national and local awards for civic achievements and garden activities. In 1997 she received the National Achievement Award from the Garden Club of America, and other national recognition has come from the Pi Beta Phi social fraternity (1998), the Daughters of the American Revolution (2010), and the Cultural Landscape Foundation (2011). In 2013, she was honored by the Foundation for Landscape Studies with its National Place Keeper Award. Locally, she was honored in 2012 by the New Orleans Botanical Garden for lifelong contributions, and in 2011 Longue Vue House and Gardens recognized her with its first Edith Stern Legacy Award for "exceptional commitment to the horticultural arts."